Every Witch Way

Ellen Dugan & Tess Whitehurst

Every Witch Way: Spells and Advice from Two Very Different Witches

Copyright © Ellen Dugan and Tess Whitehurst, 2014

Edited by Rebecca Zins

Cover art designed by Kyle Hallemeier

Stock Image: dimdimich, © istockphoto.com, 16217408

Table of Contents

EVERY WITCH WAY: SPELLS AND ADVICE FROM TWO VERY DIFFERENT WITCHES 2

EVERY WITCH WAY: TWO VERY DIFFERENT WITCHES GIVE YOU THE LOWDOWN ON THE CRAFT AS THEY KNOW IT 7

INTRODUCTION—ELLEN 7
INTRODUCTION—TESS 11

HOUSE CLEARING AND CLEANSING 16

CLUTTER CLEARING—TESS 16
HOUSE CLEANSING AND GHOSTS—ELLEN 22

KITCHEN WITCHERY 29

CELEBRATING THE KITCHEN WITCH TRADITION—ELLEN.29
A KITCHEN BLESSING 33
KITCHEN MAGICK—TESS 34

PHYSICAL FITNESS = MAGICKAL FITNESS 40

THE FIT WITCH—ELLEN 40
LOVE YOUR BODY, LIVE YOUR BEAUTY—TESS 45

THE MAGICKAL DIET 51

VEGAN, VEGETARIAN, OR CARNIVORE—TESS 51
THE OMNIVOROUS DIET—ELLEN 56

PSYCHIC AND ENERGETIC PROTECTION 61

"OUT THERE" VS. "IN HERE"—ELLEN 61
PSYCHIC AND ENERGETIC PROTECTION—TESS 66

CAN YOU BE A CHRISTIAN WITCH? 72

NO—ELLEN 72
YES—TESS 76

ANGELS AND MAGICK 82

GO CAREFULLY, MY FRIEND—ELLEN 82
ANGEL MAGICK IN THE CITY OF ANGELS—TESS 87

FAERIE MAGICK 94

WORKING WITH THE FAE—TESS 94
IF YOU CALL THEM, THEY WILL COME—ELLEN 99
A SPELL TO GENTLY REMOVE A FAERIE INFESTATION 104

PROSPERITY SPELLS 108

TAPPING INTO THE UNIVERSAL FLOW—TESS 108
A WEALTH ACTIVATION RITUAL 109

ADVANCED PROSPERITY SPELL—ELLEN **114**

PROTECTION SPELLS 119

PROTECTION PREREQUISITES—TESS **119**
AN OLD-FASHIONED GARLIC PROTECTION SPELL 123
BIG GUNS PROTECTION SPELL—ELLEN **124**

LOVE SPELLS 130

AN ATTRACTION RITUAL—TESS **130**
SMOKE SIGNAL & ROSES: AN ATTRACTION RITUAL 134
LOVE MAGICK FOR A FAMILY—ELLEN **136**

GLAMOUR SPELLS 141

FUN WITH GLAMOURY—TESS **141**
ACORN AURA OF SUCCESS CHARM 142
ROSE WATER AND WITCH HAZEL YOU-CAN'T-RESIST MIST
.... 145
THE MAGICK OF BLENDING IN—ELLEN **147**

BANISHING SPELLS 153

BANISHING UNWANTED PATTERNS WITH THE AKASHIC FIELD—TESS **153**
AKASHIC RECORD REWRITE RITUAL 154
SATURN'S DAY BANISHING SPELL—ELLEN **159**

Saturn's Day Banishing Spell 162

FULL MOON RITUALS 165

Basic Full Moon Ritual—Tess 165
Basic Full Moon Ritual 166
Full Moon Rededication Ritual—Ellen 171

"ON THE FLY" SPELLS 177

Four Fast Spells—Tess 177
Ellen's Find It Charm 178
Traffic Charm 178
Turn Your Water into a Potion 180
Decide Which Item to Purchase 181
Magick At Your Fingertips—Ellen 181
Daily Magickal Correspondences 183
All-Purpose "Magick on the Fly" Charm Verse 185

CLOSING 187
ELLEN'S BIBLIOGRAPHY 189
TESS'S BIBLIOGRAPHY 191

Every Witch Way: Two Very Different Witches Give You the Lowdown on the Craft as They Know It

Introduction—Ellen

You have your way. I have my way.
As for the right way, the correct way, and the only
way, it does not exist.
—*Friedrich Nietzsche*

Not only was this magickal book written by two witches, it was written together by two friends. And, as is the case with many friends, while we agree on numerous important things and have some hobbies in common, our lives, magickal viewpoints, and style of doing things tend to be vastly different. That's what makes it interesting!

The first time I met Tess in person was at the International New Age Trade Show in Denver. We had corresponded via email for several months after she had asked me to give her a blurb for her first book, *Magical Housekeeping*. As I adored the book and always enjoy meeting fellow authors, I was tickled to discover that we would both be attending the same trade show and promoting our new books. We exchanged phone numbers, and I gave her a call and suggested a few practical things for her to bring along, as I had been to the trade show before. Her voice was bubbly as we chatted on the phone, and her laugh was infectious.

When I was finally introduced to her at our publishing company's booth, my first thought was that I felt like a valkyrie standing next to a petite, gorgeous faerie. We looked like polar opposites as we stood there. My voice carries, and hers is soft; I am tall and curvy, she is petite and slender. At the time, I was blond; her hair was dark. It was like night and day! Excited to finally meet face to face, we started chatting and didn't stop. Later, when we had a break in our schedules, I suggested that we grab lunch. She said that she hoped they had a vegan menu at the trade show because she was a whole food vegan. That tickled my admittedly warped sense of humor so, in jest, I asked her straight-faced if that meant she ate the whole cow.

Bless her heart, she never even blinked, nor was she offended. She laughed and explained to me what her diet entailed, and as we walked toward the lunch area I remember thinking that if she passed out from hunger later, I could probably pick her up with one arm. But tiny or not, she held her own. She was clever, creative, and had a fine sense of humor—the very traits that I consider necessary in a good friend, as well as traits I admire in a Witch. Tess and I stayed in touch after the trade show and have become good friends. It is great to have another witchy writer to bounce ideas off of and talk about magickal gardens and flower folklore with, or just to commiserate with. I have come to value her opinion on both magick and energy work. Even though she and I are very different people and lead very different lives, we do share core magickal values.

Last year Tess and I were both presenters at a big outdoor author event in Florida, and we were roommates. While we sat inside our cabin talking one rainy night, we hatched the idea of writing a book together. At first we laughed because we kicked around the idea of a sweet Witch/snarky Witch theme. We argued over who would get to be the snarky Witch because honestly it was a toss-up as to who was the most sarcastic. Then we stopped laughing and realized what a unique opportunity this could be. Forget the sweet versus snarky—this was a chance to do something more spiritual and go deeper. We got down to business and started brainstorming about how we could write a book together that would tackle common questions and concerns about the Craft and address the topic of living a magickal life from both our points of view.

That conversation on a rainy night planted a seed; a few months later the idea sprouted, and then it began to grow. The information presented here is drawn from our own experiences as witches and from the wisdom gained while walking our individual magickal paths, thereby giving readers two different viewpoints for each topic. This has allowed for healthy debate that we hope will expand your horizons and help you gain both insight and knowledge of the magickal path you have chosen to walk.

Introduction—Tess

Each tradition (expression)...whether passed down or intuitively performed, is akin to a petal of a flower. No one petal constitutes the whole; all are necessary to the flower's existence.

—Scott Cunningham

I first read one of Ellen's books when I was looking for a publisher for my first book. When you're writing a book proposal, you're always supposed to do a section on books that are similar to your book so that you can differentiate and compare. So I tracked down a copy of *Cottage Witchery*, and—after reading a number of other books on the topic with which I was less than impressed—I was delighted to discover that it was *excellent*. While similar in topic to my book, it was also quite different in a complementary way. Once *Magical Housekeeping* found a publisher (which just happened to be the same as Ellen's), I asked her if she would endorse it. She said yes, and a friendship was born.

In a lot of ways, Ellen and I appear to be vastly different. I'm a decidedly New Agey, Californian, solitude-relishing Witch, while Ellen is more of a pragmatic, Midwestern, community-fostering coven high priestess. I'm known for espousing the joy of affirmations, white light, and positive thinking, while Ellen is famous for her feistiness, irreverence, and snarky sense of humor. She prefers the tarot; I prefer the I Ching. I do yoga; she lifts weights. I lean toward minimalism; she is the queen of holiday decorations. (And so on—you get the picture.)

Still, as we've gotten to know each other, we've learned that we're actually not that different. For example, while I know that Ellen will protest me telling the world about this, she is actually one of the kindest people you will ever meet. (Just a heads-up: she doesn't realize that her sweetness is actually obvious, so don't tell her.) On the other hand, as Ellen (and pretty much everyone else who knows me) can heartily attest, I can be quite snarky myself, and in many cases "snarky" would be a kind euphemism.

Additionally, while at first glance some of our spiritual and magickal practices seem to be contradictory, we've discovered that, at the base of it all, we speak the same language. In other words, from an intuitive and energetic perspective, we generally come from the same place, even if our practice takes different forms and some of our opinions diverge. And it's the way we're similar, rather than the way we're different, that I find so exciting about this book—because when we all recognize that we are drawing on the same invisible magickal and spiritual power that underlies and characterizes all things, we can fully celebrate our diversity while also delving deeper into our craft. After all, just like snowflakes, no two Witches are alike. We find our greatest power when we allow ourselves to be ourselves, and to freely and creatively express our uniqueness through our magickal and spiritual practice.

Not only that, but (as my friendship with Ellen demonstrates to me again and again), when we share what makes us unique with each other, we can benefit from the other's viewpoint. Perhaps it will change the way we do things, perhaps not. But regardless, it will add dimension and depth to our knowledge, wisdom, and experience, while inspiring us with expansive ways of working magick and communing with the Divine.

It is our sincere wish that the various perspectives and practices in this book, presented concurrently, will provide insight into what makes you and your spiritual practice unique, and give you the courage to live that distinctive brand of magick every day—not just through your rituals but also through your relationships, your career, your art, and every single thing that you do. Because there is no Witch in the world just like you. It is only by being true to your most personal and authentic vision—while simultaneously celebrating the diversity that characterizes our planet and our human family—that you can heal and bless the world in the way only you can. Yes, it takes a healthy dose of both positivity and chutzpah, but believe us: it's worth it.

Part 1: Living the Magickal Life

*Of course there must be lots of Magic in the world,
but people don't know what it is like or how to make it.*
—Frances Hodgson Burnett, The Secret Garden

House Clearing and Cleansing

Clutter Clearing—Tess

I firmly believe that a bit about clutter clearing belongs near the beginning of any book about magic. Setting the table for a romantic dinner just won't feel right if we don't clear the junk off of it first. The dance floor at a party is never going to get rolling if it's hidden under a mess of tables and chairs. And how on earth would we expect to play a good chess game if we don't first reset the board and start anew?

An ancient and oft-quoted principle of magick is "as above, so below," which you might say can be defined as meaning "the inner world reflects the outer world and vice versa" or that "form is a physical representation of spirit, just as spirit is a nonphysical representation of form." With this in mind, consider that the junk in our physical environment—the stuff that we don't love, don't use, and don't need—represents junk in our nonphysical environment, or stagnant and stuck energy in our magical flow.

Now, for witches who are concerned with manifesting positive life conditions in every area of our lives, this simply will not do. Working magick in the most harmonious possible way, after all, is a holistic science. Yes, you *can* do the equivalent of a magical shot of espresso and activate a certain intention in a pinch, but the kind of magick that brings holistic success—ongoing, sustained positivity to every life area—is a habitual lifestyle rather than a one-time event.

An important aspect of cultivating a magical mindset is thinking about everything in terms of energy, and I mean *everything*: thoughts, emotions, people, rocks, trees, houses, cities, groups, garbage, art, knick-knacks, sounds, everything. This means that *you* are a pattern of energy, and the pattern of energy that is you has a natural and ideal expression—a way that it wants to manifest and be expressed, just like a river, a sunrise, or a tree. What's more, your true desires are not outside of this expression but are rather an aspect of it. When you get in touch with what you *really* want (rather than what you think you *should* want, for whatever reason), you get in touch with your true expression. And when you release what is not a part of your true expression—i.e., stagnation in your energetic flow, which is always mirrored in the physical world as some sort of clutter or excess baggage—you make room for your ideal essence to be expressed. In other words, in large part, magick isn't about conjuring things up or tacking things on but rather about getting the junk out of the way so that the blessings and harmonious conditions that are a natural aspect of your life expression can naturally flow and manifest into form.

Energy is movement, and movement has momentum. Once you get into this harmonious momentum, everything in your life becomes easier, including magic. So instead of fighting against the current, you're flowing with it—and the things that you desire naturally flow into your life experience as a matter of course. This will not only minimize the effort required to live the magical life, it will also be pleasant and enjoyable in and of itself. When you are in this state of ideal flow and momentum, you are moving with the universe or the Divine or All That Is (or whatever you want to call it): its energy is flowing through you, and you are embracing your true identity as a finite, temporary expression of the infinite and eternal. Co-creating with All That Is and working with an awareness and respect of the singular interconnectedness of everything, all power is available to you.

Now that I've gotten so lofty, it's kind of hard to believe that clearing the junk out of your house can really do all this, isn't it? But it can, and it will! Because form mirrors spirit and spirit mirrors form, releasing things in your home that no longer serve you will not fail to precipitate the release of things in your mind, body, and emotions that no longer serve you. That's why, if there is clutter anywhere in your life—in your home, your car, your storage space, or your work area— drop everything and clear it now.

I've done so many workshops on clearing clutter that I know what a lot of you are thinking. Here are some of the challenges and questions that I get a lot, along with my answers.

"I couldn't possibly clear it; I just haven't got the time."

Well, guess what? That's because your life is overpopulated with stuff that you don't love, and your schedule is a mirror of this. So stop the vicious circle and clear out that stagnant stuff! Turn that momentum around, align with the Divine, and make way for the magick to flow.

"How do I tell if it's clutter?"

Try holding it or touching it. Is it giving you energy or taking energy away? Is it giving you thoughts and feelings of positivity and empowerment or is it overwhelming you with thoughts and feelings of negativity and disempowerment? If it's neutral, does it make sense for you to hold on to it? Does it serve you in some way? Is it worth the real estate it's taking up in your home and your life?

"My partner has a problem with clutter, but I don't."

If you have *any* clutter anywhere—the glove compartment, a box in your closet, your email inbox—clear it out. Then continue clearing whatever clutter you have jurisdiction over until there really and truly isn't anything else for you to clear. This will often magically inspire your partner to clear—or at least will inspire *you* so much that your partner's clutter won't affect your mindset quite as much as it once did.

"Where and how do I begin?"

If you're overwhelmed, just pick a small, doable area—one drawer, one shelf, or one section of the room—and clear that. Often the energy that flows to you after you clear away the stagnation will fuel your ongoing efforts. But if it doesn't, just stop when you're done with the single area, and repeat the process again tomorrow…and the next day, and the next…until the energy is flowing like a sparkling mountain stream in sunlight.

P.S. Dirt and sticky stuff count as clutter, so be sure to clean too! And note that it's always a little more fun if you bless your cleaning supplies with magical energy by visualizing them being filled with bright white light. You can also add essential oils or flower essences if you'd like to infuse your home with their aromatherapeutic and vibrational benefits. For example, a couple drops of white chestnut essence in an all-purpose cleaner or floor wash will help create a quiet and serene vibe, while honeysuckle essence will help get stuck energy moving. And essential oils like peppermint, rosemary, lavender, eucalyptus, cedar, and lemon are all wonderfully purifying and uplifting scents.

House Cleansing and Ghosts—Ellen

For those of you who want to know the basic lowdown on ghosts, here you go. Keep in mind that often when folks are convinced they have a haunting, what they are actually experiencing is old, stale energy and trapped memories in the home. Read over this information with an open mind, and see what you can discover.

To begin with, often a house that seems haunted is simply a home filled with negativity or discordant energy. If you think you are dealing with a haunted location, your first order of business is to have the homeowners clean the house. Seriously. Stale energy is trapped energy. Dust, dirt, neglect, and clutter create a residual energy and give all that old emotional residue nooks and crannies to hide in. Bless the home with salt, water, and sunlight. Fill the home with love and laughter. These simple yet powerful ingredients often banish any lingering negativity. They are simple fixes, true, and they work very well indeed.

Discordant Energy. Easy definition: "bad vibes." This occurs when unbalanced or negative energy builds up in a location. Simple cures include cleaning house, utilizing feng shui, and family counseling. Encourage the home's occupants to clear the air—to calmly discuss their feelings and work together to change the atmosphere of their home to a positive and healthy one. Now, discordant energy can be triggered by hoarding and unbalanced emotions. The buildup of discordant or negative energy hangs heavy in the air and creates a sense of being watched. Also, if the occupants have any psychic talent and are suppressing their anger, it may cause manifestations of minor violence such as objects falling and breaking.

Poltergeists. A "haunting" where objects move about violently. Traditionally these events focus on a teenager or pre-teen with latent psychic talent. The manifestation is not truly a spirit; instead, it is a combination of the youngster's burgeoning, uncontrolled energy and psychic talents.

Etheric imprints. These are like faint echoes of the past. When strong experiences occur, the energy gets "imprinted" on the vibes of a place; these can be positive or negative vibrations. They are usually minor, but the imprint may be noticeable to a sensitive person.

Etheric recordings (also called residual hauntings). Sometimes the etheric imprints go deeper and are not only the emotions and feelings of a time but are actual events that are recorded. For example, hearing footsteps walking down the stairs or seeing a figure in the same spot doing the same thing over and over are residual hauntings. Though they appear to be "ghosts," there is no consciousness, personality, or individuality in the experience. These are merely echoes of the past, aka etheric recordings, that have been recorded and are stuck on the playback here on our plane, or physical reality, for all to see.

Disembodied dead (or a traditional haunting). This occurs when the spirit of the departed does not cross over for some reason. Some spirits are shy, quiet, and confused—and some are royally pissed off and do not understand what has happened. Their own intense emotions keep them bound to the physical world.

The two most impressive styles of haunts would be a residual-style haunt and an intelligent, or interactive, haunt. A residual haunt is believed to be activity of reoccurring or traumatic actions from past events that leave an imprint on the environment. This type is probably the most common type of haunting. Because its characteristics are similar to the intelligent haunting, people often mistake it for an intelligent, or traditional, haunting.

Like intelligent haunts, some examples of activity are phantom footsteps, sounds, images, and scents. Major differences between this haunting and the intelligent/traditional haunting are that this type of haunting is not considered to be that of a ghost and there is no interaction with the living. One theory as to why this occurs is that the energy is stored or absorbed by the site due to repetitive or traumatic events of the energy expended while such actions were performed. Similar to a tape player, the energy is stuck in the current environment. Over time, that energy builds up and is discharged, showing a replay of the event, and then the cycle starts again. Some suggest that atmospheric conditions such as storms may initiate the ghostly playback.

Secondly, we have the intelligent, or interactive-style, hauntings. This type of haunting is what most people think of when they hear the word *ghost*. An intelligent or traditional ghost *may* interact with people. The most common belief is that the ghost is connected to the place or its people in some way. Here are the traditional reasons that a ghost may be tied to the location or to the folks who inhabit the site:

> The spirit may have died suddenly and not realized that he or she died.
>
> The living loved ones are so emotionally distraught that they can't let go.
>
> The spirit is emotionally connected to or very protective of their living loved ones.
>
> The ghost may have some unfinished business.
>
> The ghost's death was a result of a traumatic event (murder, car accident, etc.).
>
> They cannot rest due to an injustice done to them such as disturbing their graves or remains.
>
> Fear of the other side or judgment.

These ghostly reasons are generally associated with voices, sounds, and physical activity such as slamming, opening, closing, or unlocking doors and windows. A strong presence, a scent, or a touch may also be experienced. People sometimes see a manifestation of the ghost in the form of an apparition or a mist. In my case, I see a person just standing there smiling at me—who then disappears in front of my eyes.

Here are some things to consider when dealing with a haunting:

> If you are naturally empathic or psychic or are a magickal practitioner, well, then, wake up! You've been working to become more sensitive to the astral plane… guess what comes along with that? *You little ghost magnet, you.*

> Psychic sensitives: be smart and don't overreact to hauntings. It is the way you are, so learn to deal with it. As a psychic sensitive, you will always get a front-row seat to the show of a residual-style haunt because you will keep sensing, hearing, or seeing the playback.

> If you are a psychic sensitive or a clairvoyant, then you need to work on desensitizing yourself to the particular problem area in your (or someone else's) home. Try acknowledging the memory. Say something out loud like this: "I acknowledge your memories. Go find peace and be at rest."

> Nobody panic. Be cool. When you are confronted by this type of situation, you should react in a calm and controlled way—especially if you are a Witch or a paranormal investigator. People around you will take their cues from you and react accordingly. If the Witch is standing strong and confidently while everyone else is panicking over a manifestation, it makes other folks wind down.

Finally, consider this: as psychics and Witches, this paranormal scene is a part of our world. Not every Witch is a ghost buster, but if you choose to be a paranormal investigator, then be a voice of calm reason during investigations, and show others there is nothing to fear. You are a role model. So do your homework, study up, and act accordingly. One of the best books I have found on this topic is *The Ghost Hunter's Survival Guide* by Michelle Belanger.

You may also find it helpful while dealing with a "haunting" to cleanse the home by working my banishing spell in part II.

Kitchen Witchery

Celebrating the Kitchen Witch Tradition—Ellen

The term *Kitchen Witch* has undergone a transformation in the past few decades. Calling oneself a Kitchen Witch back in the '90s meant that the individual was a hearth-and-home practitioner—a Witch who used household tools and quietly worked magick primarily with herbs and spices found in the kitchen cupboard. Kitchen Witchery also encompassed a style of culinary magick where the magick was added to dishes and food for family and friends. It was a simple and useful style of witchery that was respected and used practically every day. Fast forward to today, and the term *Kitchen Witch* can have a vastly different meaning.

Recently I have noticed the term being used as a sort of sad code for individuals who have had to go underground, hiding their magickal practice from family and friends. I overheard someone say, "Sally went underground. Her partner found out about the big W and freaked, so she went Kitchen Witch." This comment was whispered in a conspirator's tone to another woman, and her response was a sad sigh and an "oh, poor thing" comment.

This got me to thinking. I started asking about the term and people's definitions of it at various festivals that I attended in different parts of the country. To my surprise, the term *was* considered outdated and used almost as if to denote a sort of second-class magickal citizen. Seriously? I find that to be a little disappointing. Let's be honest here: most of us are found whipping up a little magick in the kitchen from time to time. Throughout history, the kitchen held a place of honor in the home. Today the kitchen is the heart of the home, and one of the most popular rooms in the house. We gather around the table to eat and for family meetings, and at a party everyone gravitates to the kitchen. We all have sat down at the kitchen table to pay the bills, and our kids do their homework seated at the same kitchen table or perched on stools at the breakfast bar.

I think the time has come to reclaim this title as one of honor. After all, a Kitchen Witch is a down-to-earth style of magickal practitioner—one who works their magick in a practical way with the herbs, spices, supplies, and tools that they have on hand. What many folks do not realize is that this *is* a traditional form of the Craft. Back in the day, practitioners of the Craft kept a very low profile. They quietly went about their business of tending a home, growing their kitchen gardens, caring for their animals, and raising a family. Spirituality was earthy, natural, and a part of their everyday life. The use of everyday items as magickal tools was both clever and practical.

For example, the one good kitchen knife was also the magickal knife. The broom that was used to sweep the floors clean also swept out negativity and could double as the ceremonial staff. The cauldron used for cooking stews, soups, and meals was also the magickal cauldron for brews and potions. The herbs drying from the beams in the ceiling, the flowers and plants growing in the garden—everything this practical Witch put their hands on with intention was *magick*. This is what we used to call Kitchen Witchery. It's the practical, natural magick of hearth and home.

Truthfully, there are a lot more of these types of home-based Witches out there than you'd think. Modern

Kitchen Witches are mysterious, adaptable creatures. They are whispered to be domestic goddesses or gods, as in they live their magickal lives quietly, raise their families, maintain charming homes, and have successful jobs. These Witches are simply regular folks who practice the Craft in a matter-of-fact, discreet, and practical way. And what, may I ask, is so ghastly about that? Haven't we all grown up enough as a community to embrace the idea of diversity? Being a real Witch does not require a lot of drama or intrigue—or a black velvet cape.

Today Witches can be whoever they want to be. They may identify themselves by many different titles and practice whatever form of magick they prefer. Truthfully, Kitchen Witches are natural Witches who live their lives by quietly observing the magick of the natural world. They tune in to and experience the energies of the changing seasons. They tend and care for their families, pets, gardens, and homes with power, flair, and—most importantly—with an incredible type of practical, magickal intention.

No matter how you choose to identify yourself, the truth is you should just go about your life practicing your Craft and walking your own individual path in the best way that you can. For some folks, the focus of their magick is going to be in the heart of the home. Witches are walkers between the worlds. Is it so hard to imagine that they would quietly go about their business without a lot of fuss or drawing attention? That only shows how adept they are. Sometimes the most magickal thing you can do is to go about your life quietly, making a difference just because you can.

A Kitchen Blessing

Light a white candle and repeat the following charm. Allow the candle to burn out in a safe place.

The kitchen is my home's beating heart,
From here I work my magickal art.
Conjuring with spices and herbs and love to share,
This space is blessed by water, earth, fire, and air.

For more spells, charms and correspondences on the topic of Kitchen Witchery, please read the "Kitchen Cupboard Conjuring" chapter in my book *Cottage Witchery: Natural Magick for Hearth & Home*.

Kitchen Magick—Tess

Lovelock's Gaia Theory provides a scientific model for what many of the ancients knew to be true: the earth (along with everything on it) is, in fact, a single self-regulating organism. Indeed, as components of this organism, we owe our continued daily survival to countless natural conditions, beings, and ecosystems, from the plants, sunlight, soil, and rain to the people who drive the produce trucks and stock the grocery store. Remembering this interconnection regularly and acting with an awareness of it keeps us in a state of grateful awe, which in turn lends itself to earth-loving choices and a general feeling of harmonious well-being. And what more literal, constant reminder of earthly interconnection is there than the food we eat?

With all of that in mind, let's explore some magickal, earth-loving ways of approaching the preparation and consumption of food.

Sacred (Counter) Space

As I'm constantly telling my feng shui clients, if you want to experience something, first *create the space* for it to occur. For our present purposes, this means that if you want to work magick in the kitchen, you must first create a magickal kitchen! Start by clearing out all the extras (see the previous section on clutter clearing) and cleaning. The stove, in particular, symbolizes the wealth and sustenance of the household, so make it sparkle and shine! And you'll also want to give yourself every possible inch of that much-coveted counter space. A good rule of thumb is that if you don't use it every day (or almost every day), store it somewhere other than the counter.

Mood Lighting

Lighting that's warm and cozy is ideal, but you also want to make sure that you can see what you're doing. One design feature that I highly recommend is lighting beneath the cupboards and over the counter. This illuminates the dark spaces in an attractive way and sheds light on your workspace without blasting excessively harsh light all over everything. If you don't have the time, money, or inclination to pay for recessed lighting in this area, you might discreetly tack a strand of white twinkle lights beneath the cupboards, and then simply plug them in when you're preparing food or anytime you'd like to create a soothing and uplifting ambiance.

Divine Design

To enhance the magickal vibration in your kitchen—and, subsequently, your food—choose décor imagery that brings the sacred front and center in your awareness, particularly sacred imagery that's aligned with earthy nurturing and sustenance. There are a number of types of images that could fit these parameters, but here are a few examples to give you an idea; choose from these images or come up with your own.

> Sunflowers, which are aligned with the life-giving sun as well as prosperity and sustenance. They're also the source of nutritious seeds and cooking oil!
>
> An orchard in fruit, which is aligned with the Roman goddess Pomona and provides a reminder of the sweet, abundant blessings of the earth.
>
> An earth goddess such as Gaia (the primordial earth goddess of Greek mythology) or Ceres

(Roman goddess of the grain and agriculture) to remind us to be grateful that we are so perfectly loved and perfectly provided for, and to keep our prosperity flowing.

Gathering with Love

For the overwhelming percentage of the time that our species has been present on earth, whether cultivated or wildcrafted, we have gathered our food directly from the earth herself. Almost all of our ancestors (albeit not usually our most recent ones) knew exactly where and how their food grew. Since their food was actually their neighbor, they didn't have to consciously cultivate an awareness of interconnection: it was naturally built-in. Now, of course, while some of us lucky people grow at least some of our own food, most of us rely on other people to grow, pick, transport, prepare, and package the majority of the food we eat.

Once we're mindful of this disconnect, we can consciously build a bridge back to our food by simply taking a moment to consider where it came from and how it was raised, and by seeking out food that was grown and treated with the highest possible respect for the earth. This means buying local and organic whenever possible (possibly from farmers' markets), as well as looking on labels to make sure that we're not purchasing GMOs (genetically modified organisms), which are potentially dangerous to the planet and our health.

As a bonus method of honoring our beloved Mother Earth (and all the sustenance she provides for us) and fostering a healthy relationship with the food that we eat, we can educate ourselves about how produce is grown, what is best for our bodies, and what petitions to sign and causes to support. There are a number of excellent documentaries on this subject, including *Food, Inc.*, *Forks Over Knives*, and *GMO OMG*. Additionally, the last section in the book *The Botany of Desire* (the section on the potato) also provides useful insight to the frighteningly widespread practice of genetic engineering.

Conscious Preparation

Saint Therese of Lisieux said, "We cannot all do great things, but we can do small things with great love." Similarly, I don't usually prepare anything too fancy, but I do prepare simple beverages, snacks, and meals with consciousness and great love. I also like to be aware of the magickal and metaphysical properties of the ingredients I use, so that I can awaken their intrinsic magick while also letting it fuel the tide of my intention. For example, when I pour boiling water over black tea, I like to be aware of the rush of energy that moves through the water like a powerful little explosion of light. Or when I sprinkle cinnamon on my oatmeal, I like to be aware of the grounding, sustaining energy of the oats being activated and enhanced by the wealth and luxury-drawing herb. And while baking, I like to burn a natural, unscented candle to symbolize spirit merging with the physical and infusing my cookies or muffins with divine positivity and love.

Then, of course, there is the simple blessing of the food during or after preparation. For this, I might simply place my palms on either side of it and direct a feeling of love and a visualization of light toward the food, thinking or saying something like this:

Great Goddess, thank you for this food. Please bless it with love.

May I/we absorb its nutrients and positive energy thoroughly and well.

Physical Fitness = Magickal Fitness

The Fit Witch—Ellen

A little over a year ago, I joined a gym. Like most middle-aged women, I was dealing with the dreaded menopause weight gain, and I had decided that the gym held all the answers to easy weight loss. I invested in a trainer, so I could learn how to use all that shiny equipment and safely learn how to lift weights. I figured in six months I would be a totally different woman and have to buy a whole new wardrobe due to my amazing thinness. Then I got a wakeup call.

My trainer looked me in the eye and announced, "Brace yourself: we are going to be doing strength training."

I admit, I had no freaking idea what "strength training" entailed, and as my trainer continued his speech about adding more protein in my diet, my current body shape, and how my body would change, he then dropped a bomb and told me straight out: "Ignore the damn scale. This is strength training. Your weight will change slightly, but you are going to add muscle—and Ellen, muscle weighs more than fat."

Yeah, okay…internally I thought *pfffft!* What does some twenty-year-old know anyway? I would work out so hard on my own between my sessions with him that I would lose a ton of weight. I'd show him. So I smiled, I nodded, and I threw myself into the experience in typical Virgo fashion. In other words, I obsessed about the gym and working out.

I overdid my workouts. I strained my knees. I fought back from that injury, and then I became addicted to the endorphin rush. I exercised way too often and for too long. I *knew* I could lose more weight—what did that "elite status" trainer know, anyway? Then, after a few months of agony, I confessed to my trainer the extent of the muscle pain I was in, which was severe.

After a blistering lecture from my trainer—seems I never gave my muscles time to rebuild or recover…who knew—I started over and cut back on the speed and frequency of my workouts. For a few weeks, every time I entered the gym all the other trainers were giving me the hairy eyeball. Damn, they were watching and reporting back to my trainer. It was like the gym police!

So I swallowed my pride and behaved myself. In a few weeks, the pain I had been living with began to subside, and I was rewarded by my trainer with learning how to deadlift. What a rush! Slowly, as I began to strength-train smarter, I started to notice new muscles showing up in my arms, back, abdomen, and legs. It was then I realized why folks say that fit and healthy is the goal, not skinny. It is so true.

But an interesting thing happened during this past year of learning the correct, or maybe I should say *saner,* way to work out. As my body shape radically changed and my muscles began to tone, I not only became physically stronger, but my magick grew stronger as well. My spellwork became more streamlined and more powerful. Now when I worked my spells, I got better, more robust results. Also, since I felt better, I was more relaxed and focused when it came time to work my magick. This was awesome!

I started talking to other Witches about the results I was experiencing—not the body-shape results, the *magickal* results. To my surprise, I met with a lot of resistance and condescension. Yes, Pagans and Witches tend to be a full-figured community; however, the minute any Witch starts talking about weight loss or physical fitness, folks pucker up. Seems like there was a reverse prejudice going on. How dare a Witch focus on losing weight or talk about getting in shape? A bit of recreational tai chi or a smidgen of yoga here and there, walking around the festival grounds or the occasional celebratory belly-dancing around a bonfire seemed to be considered an "acceptable" form of Pagan exercise, but going to a gym regularly, lifting weights, and hiring a trainer? Scandalous.

Why is that, do you wonder? Look, it's not about looking like a runway model, it's about becoming healthier and stronger, no matter what your age. Truth be told, a fit Witch is less prone to psychic attack or any baneful spells cast against them. First off, it's much harder to hit a moving target; secondly, the stronger you are, the less chances that attacking energy can actually get in and do damage. Physical fitness builds confidence. A confident Witch is going to cast confident spells that will manifest quickly and create the changes they were designed for in a spectacular fashion. You get out of magick what you are willing to put into it energetically. Imagine what you could accomplish if you were in the best shape of your life while casting your spells!

Think about what type of exercise would be the most complementary for you. You could join a local gym, start a walking club, or take up jogging. Sign up for a martial arts class and dare to learn new things about chi (energy) and how to direct and focus it; as a magickal person that would be so interesting to explore. Learn belly dance and embrace it for the exercise that it is. Do you honestly think that the women who perform just practice for an hour a week? Ah, no. They are dedicated to their dance and take it very seriously. Also, if you are going to do yoga, then understand it for the discipline and spiritual practice that it is. The folks I know who are serious about yoga are amazingly toned, flexible, and strong.

Bottom line: no matter how you choose to work on your own physical fitness, don't play at it. Get out there, embrace change, and make yourself into a stronger, happier, and healthier Witch. The truth is, if you decide to become more physically fit, then good for you! It's not just about wanting to look good. Once you realize what it feels like to be strong, there is no turning back.

So embrace fitness and explore all the opportunities for self-improvement. Become a fit Witch and live a long, healthy, and happier magickal life!

Love Your Body, Live Your Beauty—Tess

Like the proverbial temple, your body is a place where form meets spirit. Without form, you'd be a ghost. Without spirit, you'd be a slab of meat. Together, form and spirit synthesize to create the unique energetic being that is *you*. And *everything* is energy: your body may seem solid and enduring when, in fact, it's composed of vibrating energy that, at its most fundamental level, is mostly composed of space. This means that you are literally a pattern of energy, and that within this pattern, body, mind, and spirit are inextricably interwoven.

In this day and age, even the most mainstream and scientifically minded among us know that exercising the body is one of the very best things we can do, not just for our physical health but for our emotional and spiritual health as well. From a magickal perspective, you might say that this is because it stimulates, calibrates, and decongests the energetic pattern that is our being. For example, a good brisk walk outside gets your blood pumping and your limbs moving. It fills your lungs with fresh air and brings you into contact with the sky, the earth, the plants, and the birds. As you can see, this doesn't just lower your blood pressure and burn fat; it actually activates your entire energetic being: mind, body, and spirit. With a clear mind, a radiant body, and an effervescent spirit, you are primed and ready to work powerful and effective magick.

It's About the Journey

My personal relationship with exercise has gone through a lot of phases, each of which has taught me important lessons that apply to my magickal and spiritual path. When I was a kid, I was a competitive gymnast and worked out for about fifteen hours per week. Although I didn't realize it at the time, this gave me a good experiential understanding of the principles of sacred geometry. On the other hand, it was a pretty harsh discipline for a little girl. I got a lot of injuries, and I often felt pretty bad about myself: as hard as I worked, I always felt like someone was better than I was, and it drove me crazy. And even though I was skinny, I often thought I was fat. In retrospect, although I appreciate the coordination and work ethic it taught me, it also reinforced a lot of limiting beliefs and perspectives about competition and perfectionism. Then again, perhaps the experience also helped me learn how to override these limiting beliefs more strongly than I otherwise would have.

In my twenties I was a compulsive gym rat. Although I went through brief phases of balance with regards to my body image, I now realize that I was often working out with the underlying intention to punish myself for my lack of perfection and force myself to fit into a cookie-cutter standard of beauty. Once, the day after bingeing on chocolate cake, I even worked out so hard that I drove myself to tears. I think this subtle subconscious motivation (self-punishment/perfectionism)—effectively a form of self-flagellation—is what keeps a lot of people from working out, actually. Who wants to punish herself every day? What a total drag. Unfortunately, this mindset seems to be subtly and overtly reinforced through ads and other media messages.

Finally, I seem to have gotten the message: my body is great exactly how it is right now. Still, it feels great to work out and be in shape! It's that old spiritual paradox: everything is already perfect while *at the same time* we are called to actively affect positive change. It's a paradox that's born out of the illusion of time; outside of the illusion (which is the truer truth), there is no separation of all that is, was, and will be. That is perfection. Within the illusion of time, we feel motivated to create change; that is perfection too. Although there might be changes that we desire to make in our habits or our health, the present is perfection, the future is perfection, and the time in between is perfection. A popular way that this is phrased is that "it's about the journey, not the destination" or "the journey *is* the destination." When I work out with this mindset, I feel good immediately, and that's ultimately the best motivation.

Nourished and Natural

While in the past my ideal was to be slim and trim no matter what the cost, these days I think of my ideal as being *nourished* and *natural*. I like this because rather than driving me to extremes, it reminds me to listen to my body and tune into my holistic wellness. If I eat too much for my body to digest, eat too little for my body to comfortably live on, don't work out at all, or work out until I cry, I'm not nourished or natural. Rather, the ideal of "nourished and natural" supports me in eating healthy amounts of healthy foods that replenish me and working out regularly in a way that I like and that feels good to my body.

In addition to its obvious benefits, maintaining a healthy relationship with food and exercise is an enriching magickal practice in and of itself. Magick, after all, is about being awake and alert to subtle energies and creating and maintaining positive life conditions all while being aware and respectful of the fact that everything is always changing. Maintaining a healthy relationship with food and exercise gives us a reason to practice this type of consciousness every single day. And because it counsels us to stay in communication with our body—that sacred temple that brings together the worlds of form and spirit—we stay grounded in the physical world as well as in the space between the worlds, where all magick happens.

A Few Tips and Tricks

Here are some of my favorite tips and tricks that may inspire you to nourish yourself and stay in the momentum of your natural well-being:

- If you get bored with a certain exercise regimen or you never liked it to begin with, try something else.

- Starting is often the hardest part. If you can just convince yourself to put your sneakers on and go outside (for example), the momentum is in motion, and it will feel more natural to continue.

- Doing *something* (even five minutes of exercise) almost daily is always, always, *always* better than doing nothing, plus it helps keep you in the habit.

- When it comes to dietary priorities, think veggies and fruit first, then nuts, seeds, beans, legumes, and grains.

- To encourage water drinking, get a water bottle that you love.

The Magickal Diet

Vegan, Vegetarian, or Carnivore—Tess

I was raised a meat eater, but now I'm vegan for a lot of reasons. First, because I love animals, so naturally, given the choice, I prefer not to eat them or use them for food in any way. Second, I love the planet, so naturally I prefer to choose foods that are more sustainable. Animal agriculture consumes vastly more water and land than agriculture for plant-based foods; did you know that by some calculations, not eating a quarter pounder saves as much water as not taking a shower for a year? And third, it's just plain better for you. In study after study (including the well-respected China Study and Oxford Vegetarian Study), vegetarians, and especially vegans, live longer, healthier lives. Perhaps this shouldn't be surprising since our closest relatives, other primates, usually survive mostly on leaves and other plant foods.

Now, all of that aside, I think the bottom line for me is that I would never personally kill an animal for food. I know that I don't have it in me. And if I wouldn't personally kill an animal for food, how does it morally make sense for me to pay someone else to do it for me? Interestingly, a lot of people are surprised to learn that I understand and forgive hunters more than I understand and forgive the average meat eater. Because I am convinced that the vast majority of people who eat meat would almost rather die than slaughter a pig or a cow or chop the head off a chicken. Not to mention, the animal who is killed by a hunter got to live most of his or her life out in the wild, whereas most animals who are killed in slaughterhouses live their entire lives in mind-bogglingly cramped dark cages or crates.

So, consider this: if you knew someone who raised a chicken from a chick by cutting off her beak and keeping her in a tiny, cramped box where she couldn't stretch out her wings for her entire life, you would be pretty sure that person was a psychopath. But the everyday person who eats chicken not only pays someone to do this once, but *hundreds and even thousands of times*. Similarly, would you ever in a million years watch a baby chick hatch and then throw him directly into a wood chipper simply because he was male? If you buy eggs—even organic ones—you are funding hatcheries that do exactly that. Or would you deliver a calf and then rip her away, crying, from her wailing and grieving mother again and again and again throughout that mother's lifetime so that you could drain her of her milk? If you buy milk products—even organic products—you are funding dairies that do exactly that.

In our consumer culture, we are taught not to think about these things. In many circles, simply bringing them up is seen as rude. It's even become something of a trend to share Facebook and Twitter posts about how hilarious it is to eat bacon. But as Pagans who honor the interconnectedness of all, it's our job to reclaim our conscious awareness of the repercussions of everything that we do, from the water we drink to the products we purchase to the foods we eat. Part of this is honoring other species as our equals, and certainly not knowingly or unnecessarily harming them. Another part of this is being stewards of the earth and behaving in a way that will help her to survive and thrive. Veganism is a way to do all of these things at once. More than just a super healthy diet, it's a spiritual practice.

Additionally, as a sensitive person, I have found it quite a relief to no longer be consuming the energy of fear, pain, torture, and imprisonment. The moment that I went vegan was quite an energetic turning point for me. It was right around the time that I read Karen Kingston's book *Clear Your Clutter with Feng Shui* and cleared a whole lot of stuff out of my apartment. Letting go of meat, dairy, and eggs was an extension of the clutter-clearing process when I cut away the things that were weighing me down, clouding my mind, and congesting my energetic flow. Very shortly after, I realized that I wanted to go to feng shui school and began my sacred career path, for which I still feel grateful every day.

Honestly, I understand wholeheartedly why it seems so difficult for people to make the jump into veganism: it *is* a really challenging path—not nutritionally (that part is actually pretty easy) but philosophically. Once you get honest with yourself about the lives of animals that are killed for food, living in a world that is largely unconscious about the origins of its food is hard. Knowing that the people you love would never choose to torture or imprison animals but then watching them put tortured and imprisoned animal flesh into their mouths is something you never completely get used to.

Speaking up about the way things are and then being ridiculed or shushed is also not an easy thing to live with.

At one time, keeping human slaves or not keeping human slaves was seen as a matter of opinion. There was also a time when you might say that you sided with the Nazis and not be ostracized from polite society. What changed these conditions was that a minority of brave people had the courage to speak up and say, "No, that's not okay." As Pagans, who are adept at seeing truths that other people might not yet see and who profess to view animals as our brothers and sisters, we have the opportunity to *be* those brave people when it comes to animal rights, as many of us already are. I know that no one can live a life that really and truly harms none (for example, I kill insects with my car quite frequently), but considering that witches only have one rule—do what thou wilt, harm none—we may as well do our very best to follow it to the letter.

If you'd like to learn more about the health benefits of veganism, I highly recommend the documentary *Forks Over Knives*. To shed light on the realities of factory farming and the fallacy of species-centrism, check out the films *Earthlings* and *Speciesism*. And even if you don't think you want to go vegan, being informed never hurts!

The Omnivorous Diet—Ellen

It was Erma Bombeck who said, "I didn't work this hard to get to the top of the food chain to become a vegetarian." That quote makes me giggle every time I read it. No, I am not a vegetarian, nor am I vegan. Technically I am an omnivore, meaning I choose to have both meat and vegetables in my diet. As humans, we do need to consume lean proteins in order to stay healthy and for our bodies to function at optimum levels. How you choose to ingest those proteins is completely up to you. There may be many factors to consider. For example, for folks who have soy or nut allergies, getting their protein solely from nuts is not an option. Also, you need to realize that not everyone has a vegan-friendly restaurant or specialty grocery store in their area. Many of us have to rely on what typical items are affordable and available at our local grocery stores or whatever we can grow, harvest, or hunt for ourselves.

It was once thought that eating the flesh of an animal that was harvested respectfully would help you to gain the strength, power, and spiritual qualities of that animal. For example, eggs have long been consumed, and the egg is a magickal item indeed. A perfect symbol of creation, the egg is revered as a symbol of new life and magick. Fish have been feeding humankind since ancient times, and the fish has many ties to the mythology and magick of just about every culture. Food, in all its wondrous variety, is magick. Think of the time and energy it takes to plant, raise, and harvest vegetables in your own yard. Consider the time and care a farmer lavishes on his crops. It takes effort, skill, cunning, working with the elements and the seasons, and a bit of luck to successfully harvest our foodstuffs. Food is energy and divine magick all rolled into one.

Everyone has a strong opinion on the magickal diet. It all comes down to a personal preference. As to why I will continue to eat meat, I have personally found that eating lean meat after I have worked intense magick or performed many hours of psychic readings helps to ground me. It works every time, and the protein from the lean meat helps raise my blood sugar levels and keep them on an even keel. As I have been actively working on strength training for the past year, I have chosen to continue to include lean protein in my diet. Protein builds muscles, and as I have a nut sensitivity, I'm all about the poultry these days.

Also, I discovered years ago that having meat in my system does help me build and maintain stronger emotional and energetic boundaries. For those who bemoan the fact that I am cutting off my psychic sensitivity by consuming meat, my argument is this: I prefer to keep grounded. Seriously, I'm sensitive enough psychically as it is. I don't need to be wide open to every bit of psychic energy that is out there. Yikes!

However, no matter what choice you make with your diet, you have the right to choose for yourself, and so does everyone else. I will confess that it drives me up the wall to hear someone pontificate about how they are so fabulous because they chose to give up gluten or meat or dairy. That's nice. Maybe you should just be thankful that you have the choice to decide what you wish to eat. Food allergies and other sensitivities such as lactose or gluten can limit your dietary choices. Many folks with severe allergies don't have your options. You don't hear a lactose-intolerant person bragging that it's been five years since they gave up ice cream...they are usually too busy searching for a tummy-friendly alternative.

As Witches, we are supposed to be tolerant. We should support each other in our dietary choices and restrictions even if they don't match up to our own. I've been out with vegan friends at restaurants and watched (and helped) them carefully choose items in a place where the waitress didn't even know what being vegan meant! (Tess and I still laugh about that.) Also, it's always a thrill to be at a gathering or eating out at a restaurant and then breaking out in hives, making you rush for the Benadryl—or, heaven forbid, have to use an epi-pen because there was an allergen hidden within your dish. That will make you aware of food allergens and become a label reader on a whole new level.

The magickal diet is all about choice and perspective. So let's get some perspective, shall we? Let's all decide to respect the rights of individuals to choose their diet, whether they are omnivores, pescetarian (meaning they will eat fish or seafood but not other animals), vegetarian, or vegan. All I am saying is that I don't want to be lectured or glared at if I enjoy some grilled chicken. I certainly don't roll my eyes when my vegetarian friends choose a salad or eggplant parmesan. Maybe instead of picking at each other so much, we as a community should stand together. It certainly wouldn't hurt any of us if at the end of the day we could all learn to support, relax a bit, and laugh together.

Now somebody pass the fruit salad. There aren't any nuts in it, are there?

Psychic and Energetic Protection

"Out There" vs. "In Here"—Ellen

Have you ever considered just how deeply your physical health affects your personal psychic protection? Today it is safe to say that, as a society, we all have stress; however, being in a constant state of high stress is exhausting. Furthermore, when people are under pressure, fatigued, upset, or just plain angry, they become more vulnerable to psychic attack from others. The reasons why may surprise you. We become more vulnerable because our aura gets worn down from the inside out. The aura—the personal energetic shield that is around the body—gets worn away by the constant internal bombardment of our own negative emotions.

Lots of Witches make the mistake of thinking only to protect themselves from what is "out there," yet they never stop to consider that what's inside of themselves may, in fact, be an even bigger problem. Look to your health, and you will be stronger psychically and physically.

So many of us have major stress in our lives. The hormone called cortisol, which the body produces when it is under pressure, can affect us in many ways. Cortisol is produced by the adrenal gland. Its main function is to increase blood sugar and aid in the metabolism of fat, protein, and carbohydrates. When the constant effects of stress and the accompanying cortisol production overwhelm you, it makes you feel poorly. Now, cortisol can only be counteracted in two ways. One is good; the other, not so good.

Here is the good way to counteract cortisol: exercising (hooray!). The endorphins that your body naturally creates when you work out counteract the cortisol, neutralizing it. So hit the gym or lace up your shoes and go for a walk. Sidewalks are free, baby! Get out there and move! Walking is one of the smartest things you can do to burn off calories, stress, and all that extra cortisol. Plus you'll feel great from the endorphins that your body made while you exercised. *Sayonara*, stress!

Here is the bad way to counteract cortisol: the consumption of sugar. Sugar is a poor option because it masks cortisol's effect, which explains why we tend to turn to "comfort food" when we are stressed out. If you do indulge in sweets to soothe your stress, it may feel like the stress goes away—but in reality it's still there. Sugar does not "fix" anything; it only masks the stress hormone.

You should know that the overproduction of cortisol (from your stress) makes you crave even more sugar and sweets. But that sugar you consume only feeds the cortisol, giving it and you a bigger "appetite" for even more sugar. So it's a catch-22. If you are stressed out all the time, then you have an overabundance of cortisol in your system, which can lead to major imbalances on both physical and psychic levels.

Continuing to focus on the "in here" angle, there is a link to your blood sugar levels, psychic work, and magick. What I find very interesting is that the symptoms of a blood sugar crash (low blood sugar) are very similar to magickal overload and psychic distress. The symptoms include confusion, feeling dizzy, lightheadedness, nausea, headaches, and irritability.

Something I discovered by accident years ago is that working powerful magick or performing many psychic readings in one day can cost you physically. For example, after doing intense readings for six hours at an event a few years ago, I was staggering. Even my publicist at the time noticed. She reached in, grabbed me by the arm, and told me I was finished for the day. She ordered me to take a break. Once I was on my feet, I realized that I had really overdone the medium-style readings; I was staggering and a little punch-drunk. The price of all those back-to-back readings was psychic distress. I squinted at the seemingly now too-bright light in the room, and it felt like everyone was shouting mentally. I picked up on everything and everyone around me whether I wanted to or not. To someone unaware of what was happening, it would seem as if they were under psychic attack, when instead what was actually being experienced was a psychic overwhelm accompanied by low blood sugar.

Hey, live and learn—or, in my case, live and relearn. I had to laugh at the irony that a non-magickal person had identified a psychic problem when I had not. I was too caught up in my readings to notice. (A little dose of humility for yours truly.) So I relaxed for an hour and ate a protein bar. Later, my publicist brought me an apple and sternly told me to drink some more water. I smiled and let her fuss at me. However, after my time-out I felt much better and got through the rest of the day only feeling tired instead of loopy.

So the next time you feel like you are having psychic overwhelm or a magickal hangover and you feel goofy, weak, and have the symptoms of low blood sugar, do not reach for the sweets. Go for protein and complex carbohydrates; those are the answer. Think bean burrito, not chocolate ice cream. The first food, with its protein and carbs, will raise your blood sugar levels safely and maintain them long term. The other food will spike your blood sugar, giving you a temporary high, but then in an hour or so you will crash again even harder, leaving you wide open and vulnerable on a psychic level. All of that is completely avoidable if you focus on your own body and your well-being.

Many practitioners are too focused on psychic protection from outside forces or a possible unknown assailant when instead they should be focused on what is going on inside their own bodies. The truth is that we all need to remember to look within as well as without.

Psychic and Energetic Protection—Tess

I absolutely, positively have to protect myself psychically and energetically on a daily basis. Indeed, as an extremely empathic Witch who lives in an urban area, beginning to do this was a turning point for me. Before I regularly began practicing what I call "magical hygiene," I was quite susceptible to a spiritual sort of depression: an unease and energetic heaviness that would seem to arise out of nowhere, attach itself to me, and negatively effect my mood, self-esteem, relationships, and energy level. After I got in the habit, while I still have my challenges and funks, of course, I am generally quite possibly one of the happiest and most enthusiastic people you will ever meet. Now when I feel my mood begin to flag, it feels like it's actually me, not some mysterious energy, that's causing that experience. Being more of a known entity, these natural fluctuations in mood feel much more endurable. They feel more like interesting opportunities to explore or take a break or look at things from a new angle and less like proof that the world is a hostile, creepy, confusing, or otherwise negative place.

My Go-To Basics

What does my magical hygiene practice entail? First and foremost, it involves working with my favorite protective ally, Archangel Michael (more about him in the angel section below), but it involves some other steps too. I like to switch it up sometimes to keep it fresh, but my magical hygiene practice will pretty much always involve the following steps:

Calling on Archangel Michael.

Asking Michael to vacuum my aura and to cut and remove any and all cords of fear and attachment, which are challenging, draining energetic relationships with people or conditions.

Asking Michael to surround me in very bright white light, then very bright indigo light, "in which only love remains, through which only love may enter."

Sending visualized roots from my tailbone deep into the core of the earth, drawing golden-white earth light up from the core and sending it throughout my body and aura. When I do this, I feel myself nestling down on the surface of the earth, almost as if this light is magnetically pulling me down.

Sending a visualized trunk and branches from the crown of my head up out of the atmosphere and into the infinite, glittering cosmos, drawing clear light with rainbow sparkles down from the heavens and sending it throughout my body and aura.

Feeling and sensing all this light as a bright sphere of positivity that completely surrounds and encompasses me, and sending it spinning gently in a clockwise direction in order to seal it into my energy field (sort of like turning a screw).

Angelic Bodyguards

If at any time I find myself in a situation where I feel physically unsafe, I immediately call on Archangel Michael, but sometimes I call on all five of the elemental angels to surround me and protect me: Archangel Raphael (the air element), Archangel Michael (the fire element), Archangel Gabriel (the water element), Archangel Uriel (the earth element), and Archangel Metatron (the fire element). I then sense and imagine these angels walking around me like a team of extremely intimidating and expert bodyguards. As you might imagine, this helps me to feel safer right away. I've found it to be quite effective.

Mirrored Sphere

Occasionally when I'm out in the world, I wish I were invisible, or at least I wish I didn't feel so self-conscious. This feeling often arises when I feel especially aware of someone watching me, but it often appears when I'm just feeling more sensitive and introverted than usual. In these cases, I'll often envision a sphere of mirrors completely surrounding me, reflecting all energy and attention right back to its source. This way, I feel completely insulated from any and all glances, including lecherous ones. When I'm in bright sunlight (as I often am in Los Angeles), I can also sense that on an energetic level, this creates a blinding ball of light that causes onlookers to avert their eyes.

Black Tourmaline

Sometimes drama happens, and you might feel like the negative thoughts and feelings of a certain person or group are pummeling you from afar. Over time, this can be very draining. If these thoughts and feelings are warranted, of course, you might need to make amends with the person or group, but if they aren't and you'd prefer not to interact with them anyway, you might simply need to protect yourself from the relentless onslaught of challenging vibes. The way I like to do this is by sleeping with a black tourmaline. It neutralizes and mitigates the effects of negativity so that I can recharge and renew in peace. If you'd like to try this, first find a black tourmaline that feels good to you. Cleanse it by running it under cool water, smudging it in white sage smoke, and setting it in sunlight for at least five or ten minutes. Then hold it in your right hand and charge it with the intention to absorb, neutralize, and transmute negativity. Then simply sleep with it under your pillow, on your nightstand, or in your hand. Once a week or so, cleanse it quickly by simply running it under cold water or setting it in bright sunlight for a few minutes.

Secondhand Silk

As a vegan, I make a habit of avoiding animal products of all kinds, except in the case of reclaimed, or secondhand, silk. Thanks to Ellen, who taught me about silk's protective properties, I began wrapping myself in it for extra psychic and emotional protection, especially in situations that in the past were all but impossible for me to withstand from an energetic perspective, namely concerts and other crowded events. (Empaths are famous for their inability to abide crowds.) By covering my heart, sacral, and solar plexus chakras, it mutes all the harsh vibrations and energies, allowing me to feel my own emotions and no one else's. Before I tried this, concerts would literally reduce me to tears; now I can hang out like a normal person and enjoy the show. (Thanks again, Ellen!)

Can You Be a Christian Witch?

No—Ellen

I am often asked about this controversial topic while I am at an author event, teaching a class, or speaking at festivals. At first I could not figure out what the fascination was with my answer, but as my quick, snarky answer never changes, and the reaction is always gales of laughter, I began to realize that folks just enjoyed hearing me say it. *Can you be a Christian Witch?* My standard answer is, "Can you be a Baptist Jew? No, you can't. So get off the fence—it's one or the other."

Oh my, I have probably just offended someone. Well, *I* get offended when some chick in a white eyelet sundress wearing Halloween-costume fairy wings and sporting a big crucifix around her neck stands there simpering at me, wanting me to assure her that she won't go to hell just because she is dabbling with a bit of Witchcraft. After all, she just loves faeries and magick. It's all so pretty…but she can still be a Christian, right? Don't forget, she has lots of magickal books; they are so cool. Plus she has seen every episode of *Charmed*. Good grief.

In my opinion, no, you cannot be a Christian Witch. Why? Because Witches are following a polytheistic religion. We believe in and worship more than one god; we believe in the god and the goddess and the many faces thereof. We believe in karma, in reincarnation, and that our actions in this life are important. We are not "forgiven" for any misdeed; instead, we know that we are responsible. Witches work hard on maintaining their magickal neutrality. We embrace the sacredness of life and of nature, communing with spirits and believing that prophecy and visions are, in fact, not only real but a part of our spiritual rights as humans. Also, Witches do not believe in proselytizing; we do not recruit or convert others.

There is no fear in the Craft, but it seems to me there is a very real fear at the core of Christianity—the fear of divine retribution from an angry, jealous, and vengeful god. Before someone accuses me of Christian bashing, I invite you to research the history of the church's conversion of the masses. Countries, territories, and entire races of people were converted by force or they died. Anyone who was different or worshipped differently was branded a heretic and met with an unfortunate end. There is a long, bloody, and violent history to Christianity. Even the crucifix is a symbol of torture and suffering. Roman Christian soldiers emblazoned it on their shields and banners as they moved into and conquered new territories. This was a way to advertise just what would happen to the people if they did not fall into line. Let's be honest here, in ancient times the common folk could not read, but they understood what that symbol meant when they saw it: death by crucifixion.

And don't get me started on the burning times, also known as the women's holocaust. While the numbers of the victims vary from several hundred thousand to millions, depending on who you ask, it is true that across Europe many lost their lives from being accused of practicing Witchcraft. The bottom line is those atrocities were real. The torture and murder of women, men, and children all to save their souls in the name of Christianity is sickening.

Still think you can be a Christian Witch? Then again, I invite you to take a realistic and honest look at the guidelines of Christianity. Divination, visions, a belief in reincarnation, communing with spirits, any sort of magick, and, of course, the belief in more than one god and/or a divine feminine is frowned upon most strongly, which is a nice way of say it is *forbidden*. There, in a nutshell, is your answer. You cannot claim to be both a Christian and a Witch when these two belief systems are in such direct theoretical opposition from one another.

I do respect other spiritual paths. We could all stand to have an open, honest dialogue with each other. However, I am standing by—and standing up—for my spiritual beliefs. As an author, I am in the unique position of having had the opportunity to meet different sorts of magickal folks from all over North America. That whole wanna-be-Witch-chick-in-the-white-sundress scenario really happened, and I get hit up with variations of this question almost daily. How would you feel if you were confronted with that on a regular basis?

While I appreciate that Witches are so popular in our culture, thanks to television and fiction, the truth is that Witchcraft is a spiritual practice—and one that should be respected, not played with. There is nothing more dangerous than a magickal dabbler. People who play with the Craft because they think it's romantic or cool typically cause chaos. It annoys me to no end for folks to take my religious practices and turn them into what they imagine is a sort of fun hobby because they are looking for a thrill.

You do not get to have this both ways. Embrace the spirituality of the Witch wholeheartedly or stick with your own religion and stop playing with the Craft. Witches know that our spiritual path is not for everyone, nor should it be.

Yes—Tess

Here's why I believe that you can indeed be a Christian Witch: when it comes to spirituality, I absolutely refuse to subscribe to rules regarding what names you can and can't call yourself, and what those names may or may not mean to the world. I belive we've had quite enough of that as a culture. Not to mention, there are as many ways to be a Witch as there are Witches. And since spirituality is an utterly, utterly personal thing, I believe that there are also as many ways to be a Christian as there are Christians.

Joseph Campbell said, "Every religion is true one way or another. It is true when understood metaphorically. But when it gets stuck in its own metaphors, interpreting them as facts, then you are in trouble."

By "trouble," I assume that he means everything from petty squabbles to discrimination to violence and even war and murder, which are all ridiculous ways to behave when what you're really at odds about is a metaphor for the Divine. And the way I see it, saying you can be *this* but then you can't be *that* is a symptom of getting stuck in metaphors and interpreting them as facts.

And so, yes, by many conventional definitions of the words "Christian" and "Witch" (of which there are many), I understand that it might not make sense to say that you're both at the same time. But I am not interested in conventional definitions. I am interested in creative spirituality: in finding what inspires *you personally* and not what someone else told you should inspire you or what a narrow definition dictates. What's more, when we're talking about the Great Mystery (one of my favorite names for God/dess), we are, to quote

Joseph Campbell again, talking about "that which transcends all levels of rational thought." So by its very definition, if we are actually talking about the Great Mystery or any way that we may interpret or celebrate the Great Mystery, it will almost definitely not make any rational "sense." (If it did, it would not be the Great Mystery. Consequently, we would be talking about something else entirely.)

Now that my philosophical rant is out of the way, I'd also like to point out that where I live (California), because of the large Mexican population, there are plenty of Catholic practitioners of something that may not always be called Witchcraft but looks pretty much like the same thing from where I'm standing. I first learned about this from my visits to botanicas. Have you ever been to one? We have them in or near just about every town, regardless of size. California towns that have no New Age bookstore will quite often have at least one botanica. If you ever get the opportunity to go to one, do! They're magical! Perhaps the first thing you'll notice is every kind of tall jar candle you can think of, from Catholic saints to Yoruban orishas to magical intention candles of countless varieties. (Please be advised that many of these candles, like "Come to Me Lover" and "Shut Your Mouth," do *not* honor the free will law and *will* come back to bite you in the butt if you burn them with the intention to manipulate another. I, uh, guarantee it…yup, definitely won't ever do that again. Honestly, I'm lucky I survived my baby Witch years relatively intact.) You'll also find herbs, statues, incense, candles, soap, rosary beads, scented waters, and pretty much any variety of spiritual or magickal supply you might need in a pinch. Often the owner of the botanica (or someone who works there) will also offer alternative healing work of some kind.

If you examine the roots of this Catholic/Yoruban/folk mixture, you'll see that, like many ancient and indigenous spiritualities during times of Christian conversion, South American folk beliefs were not completely eradicated but rather assimilated and syncretized to Christianity—in this case (because South America was colonized by Spain), Catholicism. And so, in much the same way that the goddess Brighid in Ireland is said to have become Saint Bridget and Avalon became Glastonbury, the Great Goddess of the Americas became Mother Mary and folk remedies and practices became infused with Christian iconography. The African influence found its way in into the mix too (via the Carribean), hence the orisha candles.

All of this just goes to show that as comforting as it may be to imagine that there are cleanly drawn lines between what constitutes a "Christian," what constitutes a "Witch," and what constitutes any other name you might have for any particular spirituality or cosmology, this is simply not the case. You might as well say that all Christians have to stop having Christmas trees or burning Yule logs in December, as these traditions are derived from ancient Pagan customs. You might also say that I have to stop calling on Saint Francis of Assisi every day to watch over my cats, which is something that I am absolutely not willing to do. (Incidentally, Saint Francis might be called something of a Christian Witch, although if he had declared such a thing during his lifetime, it would certainly not have gone well for him. He talked to the birds and wrote poems about the sun, moon, stars, and elements, after all.) Spirituality is fluid, words are just words, and we are all one big human family. You could get hung up on distinctions, but why?

Call yourself what you want to be called, just don't get stuck on your chosen label(s). Interweave whatever inspires you into your spiritual path, and allow others to do the same. Do what thou wilt. Harm none.

Angels and Magick

Go Carefully, My Friend—Ellen

When it comes to working magick with the angels, I approach it the same way I would handle a stick of sweating dynamite: with extreme caution and considerable care. I have cultivated this magickal point of view because over the years I have witnessed many folks who get into angel magick (usually because they figure it's somehow safer than Witchcraft)—and then I have witnessed the chaos and destruction that careless angel magick can wreak. Truthfully, angels are not the cute, cuddly, naked babies popular culture has made them out to be. They are not ethereal romantic women with long hair and a lilting Irish brogue who help you with your love life, either. Angels are another type of entity altogether, and only the foolhardy decide to work angel magick without respect and restraint. If there was ever a time for wisdom and personal control, it is now, as we contemplate the topic of angel magick.

I once literally broke a sweat when I overheard some romantic New Ager gushing over how much fun it is to work with angels: They're just so beautiful and loving. I feel so safe; why, it's like a hug from heaven. Oh, and I think The Metatron is my personal guardian angel!

By the gods, I'm starting to get a little tick under my left eye even recalling that comment. Just in case you didn't know, "The Metatron" (capital T, capital M) is *the* head angel. He is the voice of God and is associated with the top of the Tree of Life. A few of his many titles are the "King of Angels" and the "All Knowing"—he's like a super angel. The Metatron is definitely not a warm and fuzzy "personal angel," which explains my twitching over the previous statement. According to angelic lore, The Metatron is thought to manifest as a pillar of fire and is brighter than the sun. Wow. A personal guardian angel? I really don't think so... 100,000 SPF sunscreen anyone?

As a practicing Witch for over thirty years, I consider angel magick to be in the category of theurgy. Theurgy is defined as rituals that are designed to align oneself with the Divine, or the angelic realms; in other words, high magick. I have carefully researched, written about, and worked respectfully with the planetary archangels and their coordinating flowers and herbs. But are you noticing something about my descriptions? The adverbs *carefully* and *respectfully*. Angels are an incredible power source, and one that is nondenominational. They do not care what religion you are, and if you call them correctly, they come.

Here is the minimum of what you need to know about the four more commonly known archangels. I have also included the magickal correspondences that I employ.

Magickal Correspondences for the Four Archangels

Raphael. You may call for the archangel Raphael's assistance with matters of healing, personal power, information, and communication, plus the cunning and determination to make your dreams come true. This archangel has a radiating sort of energy that manifests differently for everyone, so be aware and take note on how you experience his presence. Element: air. Season: spring. Day of the week: Wednesday. Astrological association: Mercury. Tarot cards: Ace of Swords and the Magician. Color: purple. Flowers and herbs: iris and lavender.

Michael. You may call upon the archangel Michael for strength, courage, physical protection, psychic protection, truth, and divine illumination. Just a quick note here: he has a warrior's spirit and a ferocious energy. Be respectful and consider any requests made of Michael with the utmost of care. Element: fire. Season: summer. Day of the week: Sunday. Astrological association: Sun. Tarot cards: Ace of Wands, the Sun, and Strength. Colors: red and gold. Flowers and herbs: marigold and sunflower.

Gabriel. Request Gabriel's assistance to make your dreams come true. She is the angel of magick, clairvoyance, and visions. She also assists with issues of fertility, birth, and children. Gabriel can help you to overcome your deepest fears. Keep in mind that she is not always gentle with washing away your fears either. Like the element she is associated with, water has many moods. Element: water. Season: fall. Day of the week: Monday. Astrological association: Moon. Tarot cards: Ace of Cups and Queen of Cups. Colors: blue and white. Flowers and herbs: white rose and honesty (moonwort).

Uriel. Appeal for the archangel Uriel's assistance regarding practical matters of prosperity, the harvest, and gardening. Uriel is sometimes called the earth angel, and as such he is linked to the faeries and the elemental kingdoms. There is quite a debate with magicians concerning this particular archangel, so you may see a variation on the spelling of the name (Auriel) as well as a difference of opinions on the correspondences. The following are the ones I have successfully used in the past. Element: earth. Season: winter. Day of the week: Saturday. Astrological association: Saturn. Tarot card: Ace of Pentacles and Nine of Pentacles. Colors: green and brown. Flowers and herbs: honeysuckle, tulip, wheat, and corn.

Although it is not a personal practice of mine, it is not uncommon for Witches to work with four of the archangels when a magick circle is cast and the four quarters are called. Generally this would be Raphael in the east, Michael in the south, Gabriel in the west, and Uriel in the north. Also, we should consider the classic Lesser Banishing Ritual of the Pentagram, where the four archangels are called, one at each of the cardinal points, or directions. I have always found this to be a lovely and quietly intense magickal working. The LBRP is a powerful ritual for ceremonial magicians as well as Witches, and it is to be approached with reverence and used only as needed, not for every little hiccup that you encounter along your life's path.

When it comes down to it, it is your own personal preference that will dictate whether or not you work magick with the angelic realms. If you are mindful of their powers and thoughtful and considerate in how you approach their magick, you should see great results. Just remember to always give them the respect that they deserve.

Angel Magick in the City of Angels—Tess

When I began to work with angels on a daily basis as a part of my spiritual and magickal practice, it was a major turning point for me. After hearing about Ellen's experience with angels being like "a stick of dynamite," I realized that my perhaps uncommonly intense reliance on the angelic realm probably has something to do with the fact that I live in Los Angeles, the city of angels. Let me explain.

Los Angeles is where I found my magick when I was eighteen. I had just moved here from a small town to go to acting school, and I suddenly had access to magick books and all the occult wisdom and energy that was swirling around everywhere. Unfortunately, opening up to and practicing spells right away without a physical teacher or a mentor of any kind sent me into a state of treacherous openness to all forms of negativity. I had no real idea how to shield or protect myself. While I was ecstatic to discover that I was a Witch and to begin to practice the Craft, I found myself spiraling into unstable and dark times. In time, I dropped out of acting school, got in a kind of scary car accident, experienced high drama of many varieties, and generally had a pretty bad time of it.

In fact, it wasn't until I moved to the Grand Canyon a year or so later that I began to balance out and find harmony and joy again. During my stay at the canyon I spent time detoxifying in the sunshine, gazing into the silent emptiness, gathering desert sage, smudging, saying affirmations, and soaking in herbal and sea salt baths to cleanse my aura.

Then I moved back to Los Angeles, and wham! After just a few months, I was down in the dumps again, beaten down and downtrodden, negativity surrounding me like a murky cloud and following me wherever I went. I'd have times when I felt a little bit better—maybe after a sea salt bath or a workout—but then I'd find my stomach full of knots and my mood would sink back down into the depths.

It actually wasn't until I started working with angels on a regular basis that this pattern turned around for good. Every day, to this day, I call on Archangel Michael to cleanse and shield me, my home, my car, and my loved ones. I also call on a group of angels to surround my home—also every single day—and I call on other angels as necessary throughout the day for protection, healing, and all number of things. As a matter of fact, I don't sit down to write without very respectfully calling on Archangel Metatron for help with organization and laser-focused magical expression.

What does all of this have to do with Los Angeles? In feng shui, the realm of heaven (which is one and the same with the angelic realm) is also associated with transportation, the metal element, and yang (masculine/bright/fast/hot/dry/loud) energy. Seriously, can you think of a city that is more *yang* than Los Angeles? There are five-lane freeways in every quarter of the huge, sprawling, hot, blindingly sunny city, filled with fast-moving (or jammed and honking) vehicles. People, buildings, and noise are everywhere. This excessive yang energy, I believe, is what makes Los Angeles such a tricky and hard-to-master town for so many people. The energy is the opposite of mellow: it's like standing in the middle of a busy and fast-moving freeway at noon in July. You've got to be literally quick, on pointe, and on your guard—and from an energetic perspective, especially if you're sensitive, you've got to be very grounded and very shielded in order not to literally go crazy. (Believe me.)

Furthermore, the brightest light casts the darkest shadow. This is true in both the physical and spiritual sense. Los Angeles is the bright, sunshiny city of dreams: if you can conceive of something, you can probably create it here, whether it's a movie, a career, an invention, a business, a relationship, or a nonprofit organization. And very bright spiritual energy abounds in the form of gurus, healers, yogis, and spiritual locations such as Lake Shrine, the Pacific Ocean, and the Santa Monica Mountains. On the other hand, very dark energies swirl around here as well: broken dreams, earthbound spirits, cult leaders, predatory humans, exploitative business models, and pretty much any variety of juju you can think of.

The word *angel* literally means "messenger." As the entertainment capital of the world, it is literally the business of the city to broadcast messages throughout the entire planet. Is this city aptly named or what?

So, in the case of Los Angeles (which, obviously, is very different than many other parts of the world), the angelic realm is just the magical stick of dynamite you (or at least *I*) need in order to survive and thrive. Yes, angelic energy might be intense, but so is the city outside my door and under my very floorboards.

I know I've touched on some of my daily practices already, but for practical purposes, you'll find a brief overview of the way I personally work with the angelic realm below.

I call on Archangel Michael daily for help clearing and shielding me, my house, my car, and my loved ones. I also call on him for extra help throughout the day for protective purposes.

I call on Archangel Metatron for help with magical expression, organization, and clarity.

I call on Archangel Jophiel when it comes to being a devotee of the spiritual aspects of aesthetic beauty (when it comes to my home, body, and art projects, for example).

I call on Archangel Raphael for help with physical healing.

I call on angels (of any identity) to surround my home with a circle of protection daily and to watch over my and my boyfriend's cars. (Cars and transportation are in alignment with the angelic/heavenly realm in feng shui.)

Here's an example. I once called on Archangel Michael and his band of mercy to walk beside me as bodyguards when I found myself in an empty alley behind my apartment building, walking by a seemingly violent man yelling to himself and explosively punching trashcans. On my way back home, a police car drove slowly by (which I had never seen before in that area) just at the exact same moment and point in space that I discovered the man crouched behind a car, apparently waiting for me to pass back by so that he could pounce. The cop glared at the man, and the man slumped dejectedly and walked away as I let myself safely back into my apartment complex. I was like, "Wow, *thank you*, Michael!" (Archangel Michael is the patron saint of police officers, in case you didn't know.)

Faerie Magick

Working with the Fae—Tess

If you've ever met me, it's likely you've noticed that I'm part faerie. When I encounter psychics and energy healers, the first words out of their mouths are often, "You have a strong connection to the faeries…" (And I'm like, "You don't say!") Indeed, although I've been obsessed with any reference to faeries for as long as I can remember, it was the springtime of my fourteenth or fifteenth year that I first consciously felt their call. I think it was the wildflowers in the vacant lot behind my apartment building that communicated my alignment with the realm of the fae. The message came through as an intense interest in the subject, and I went to the library and checked out every book about faeries that I could find. At Halloween of that same year, I found some faerie wings in a drugstore and wore them to school every day for some time (even for my junior year class photo).

When I discovered my fascination, my mom expressed that she had always been interested in faeries as well. A tiny woman of Irish and English descent with huge dark eyes and long black hair, my mom inherited her love of wildflowers and herbs from her Irish father, who was a gardener by trade. All of this contributes to my belief that I am, in fact, descended from the faerie people. This isn't quite as farfetched as it may sound. In Ireland and England, for quite some time, it was understood that the faeries were a race of magickal folk who may or may not have been human. (They may have been the Picts, the Tuatha de Danaan, or simply those who still followed the old religion of nature.) For centuries, certain families were believed to literally have faerie ancestry somewhere in their family tree.

Nevertheless, if you research faeries in a well-rounded way, you'll find that there is simply no ultimate authority on what they are exactly or precisely how one might go about working magick with them—and that's just the way they like it. Like the butterflies and dragonflies with whom they sometimes cavort, they really aren't fond of being pinned down. Still, over the years I've developed certain "*fae*losophies"—nothing set in stone, mind you, just general feelings and impressions about the fae and how we as Witches can interact with them.

Showing up in some capacity in ancient cosmologies across the globe, faeries may be thought of as the aliveness and consciousness of nature. This includes the plants, flowers, trees, air, wind, sunlight, fire, rain, snow, lakes, rivers, oceans, animals, and the earth beneath our feet. And as far as we may have culturally diverged from the awareness of this, *we* are, in fact, a part of nature as well. So this jives with the concept that faeries are mythical humanlike beings, first because everything does have a consciousness, just like we do, so (for example) thinking of the consciousness of the air as tiny winged humanoids isn't too far off, especially as reality is a lot more fluid than modern sensibilities tend to recognize (but also because this psychologically reminds us of our true kinship with the wind). Second, because there was a time when humans were just as natural, free, and aligned with the wisdom and power of the earth as wild animals are today. As this shifted into a more separate existence, it makes sense that the actual humans of the olden times may be present in the cultural consciousness as something akin to mythical faerie beings.

Of course, we Witches of today engage in practices that realign us with these ancient ways of wildness and wisdom. So, in a sense, all magick is faerie magick in that it's a rekindling of our ancient relationship with the aliveness of each aspect of nature as well as the unified consciousness of all nature, of which we are a part. Still, specifically calling upon and working with the faeries adds a certain flavor to one's magick, not to mention that this is what modern Witches generally mean when they talk about "faerie magick."

Here are some of the practical ways that I like to work with the realm of the fae.

Flower Communication

When I wrote *The Magic of Flowers*, I spent a good amount of time outside, simply listening to the wisdom of flowers. And I still love to do this! It tunes me right in to the conscious, living wisdom of blossoms and the entire natural world, and it is as if faeries are whispering to me and filling me with healing energy and love. To communicate with a blossom, simply go outside, stand or sit near a blossom, relax your body, and simply gaze at the blossom with a relaxed openness. While it's ideal to leave space in your mind and body for the wisdom of the blossom to make itself known to you, it's also ideal to do this with a very relaxed attention and expectation. Just like faeries themselves (or like dolphins or dogs or cats), the wisdom will be much more likely to be drawn to you if you are not pursuing it but rather are sitting in receptive appreciation.

Butterfly Dance

As natural winged creatures of beauty and transformation, butterflies are literally faeries. Already twice this year, a butterfly has chosen to flit around me as I took a walk. And when this happened, both times, I spontaneously felt like dancing to the rhythm of his flutter. Try this if you're ever in a similar situation and notice the glimmering faerie energy it confers.

Cat Worship

We all know that the Egyptians worshipped actual cats. But did you also know that in many parts of Britain, cats were considered actual emissaries of the faerie realm? Indeed, if you take a moment to tune in to your feline friend, you will notice that this wild spirit of nature's decision to live indoors with humans has not diminished her wildness or her power one bit. As devotees of our cats (and let's not deceive ourselves, that's certainly what we are! Owners? Pshaw!), we can honor this wildness and power, and help realign ourselves with it, by tuning in deeply with what our cat most desires, from a pet to a treat to a good brushing, and then giving it to her. And then doing this again and again, every single day, like good little devotees.

If You Call Them, They Will Come—Ellen

The topic of faerie magick is a popular one with Witches. Typically the individuals who work most often with the elemental realms and the Fae are earth Witches, but anyone who practices garden magick, herbalism, or who grows a garden learns to develop an appreciation for the nature spirits. Faeries are wildly popular with children, and often folks mistakenly assume that faerie magick is safe to teach to their kids. I have found from personal experience that this is actually the exact opposite. Back in the day when my children were small

I taught my youngest, my daughter, faerie magick. Wow. We had some crazy goings-on until I realized my mistake, sat down with my daughter, and explained to her why faerie magick has to be respected. Then it took time and effort to encourage the Fae out into the garden and not to run amok inside of our home. (After all, I had called them in, so I had to be the one to encourage them to go back outside.)

Over the past thirty years I have heard similar stories, typically when Witches sit down and start trading war stories of spells gone awry or magickal lessons learned. I once had someone approach me who was absolutely convinced that she had malevolent spirits in her home. As she described the problems, I worked hard to keep a straight face. It wasn't that I thought she was joking, but because what she described was similar to what I had encountered myself as a young Witch when I had invited faeries inside of my own home. Long story short, those little buggers wreaked havoc, and it was a hell of a learning experience for me. Twenty years later, the story is very amusing; at the time we experienced all of the trouble, it definitely was not!

So I finally asked her if she had taught her little ones faerie magick; she admitted that she had. I asked her if she had considered the possibility that a faerie infestation, not angry ghosts, was causing a ruckus in the home. I gently pointed out that if she was working with the elemental forces and had taught the kids how to call on the faeries, maybe she needed to think about this from a whole different angle. After all, if you keep calling the faeries and elementals in during rituals, eventually *somebody* will take you up on the invite.

Faerie Infestation: Things to Watch For

> Missing everyday small objects—as in you just put it down, turn around, and the object disappears, only to show up someplace else in a very unusual spot. (Such as keys, coins, and small pieces of jewelry.) If you find yourself laughing and wondering "what in the world?"—that's a big clue!

> A sense of mischief and laughter in the air when you realize that the everyday objects are missing.

- A house that never feels at rest, even after the kids are down for the night.

- Pets that happily chase "nothing" all over the house or who play with something that you cannot see.

- A baby or toddler that laughs at nothing and seems entertained by something *only they can see*. (There will be a feeling of sweetness around the child if the Fae are nearby; they enjoy watching over children.)

- If you or guests see movement out of the corner of your eye that is low to the ground. We are talking broad daylight here, with all pets accounted for.

- Hearing booms and crashes, walking into the room where the sound came from, and finding nothing out of place at all. Then the noise is in another part of the house, and the more you look, the less you find. You may feel like you are being tricked or teased, but you will *not* feel threatened.

- Mushroom circles growing on your property on a regular basis. Not once a year, but all the time.
- Unusual growing patterns in your garden plants such as plants blooming out of season, blooms that morph double, or flowers that change color for no reason.

These may be signs that faeries are involved. Remember, faeries and nature spirits are attracted to magick users, children, nature, gardens, and pets, so you may be a magnet for them. If your kids practice magick, be sure they are not calling the faeries in "just for fun." I have seen it happen many times.

If you feel you need to calm things down in your home, or if things get out of control, then leave some gifts out in the garden for the faeries and invite them to move outdoors, where they belong. Even if you live in the city and do not have a garden, leave a token for the Fae outside. Plant some pots of flowers or herbs and invite the faeries outdoors to guard over them. The Fae will be happy to tend the plants outdoors and watch over your home from the outside. (For more information on dealing with faeries in the home, check out my book *Garden Witchery*.)

My best advice for faerie infestations is to laugh, smile, and relax. Make sure to tell the nature spirits that you appreciate all their work protecting the home and family, and then politely but firmly encourage them to go outdoors. Here is a spell to help you do just that.

A Spell to Gently Remove a Faerie Infestation

Gather together some pretty baubles that you are willing to leave outside forever. Once you gift them to the faeries, you *cannot* take them back. Items that the faeries appreciate include crystal points, shells, smooth beach pebbles, decorative garden stakes, and, of course, flowering plants in the garden or containers. Take the gifts to the garden and display them on a little stepping stone or tucked into a container of flowers. Then, at a 'tween time (sunrise, noon, sunset, or midnight), repeat the following verse:

Elementals, Fae, and faeries dear,
Yes, it is true I have called you here.
Return all my missing items by the end of the day,
I offer prettier gifts that are only for your play.
I ask you to return to the garden where you belong,
I make this request with respect, as I wish you no harm.

Work this magick with love and respect, and remember to thank the faeries and elementals for their time and attention. That should fix you right up in a twinkling!

Part II: Spells, Enchantments, and Charms

"What you dream, you can grow."
—*Alice Hoffman, Green Witch*

Prosperity Spells

Tapping into the Universal Flow—Tess

Mother Earth is naturally suited to amply provide for everyone's needs. But let's face it: our current economic setup leaves much to be desired. Built into our money system is the idea that natural resources and even our precious everyday moments must be transformed into products and sold. What's more, while this is an abundant and generous universe and we are by nature a compassionate species, our mainstream cultural beliefs surrounding money are based around wastefulness, exploitation, and the idea that more for you means less for me (and vice versa).

I only point all of this out because in order to overcome the pervasive limiting beliefs that stem from our present cultural climate, we must first recognize and acknowledge them. Once we do that, we can work magick that helps us transcend them. Doing so not only helps transform our own expectations and experiences but also, on a vibrational and energetic level, subtly yet palpably helps to transform the very fabric of our culture's prosperity consciousness, and this helps *everybody*. Because one of the core principles of magick is "what we send out [energetically] comes back to us multiplied," magick performed on this global level reaps personal benefits that are exceptionally powerful and long lasting.

With all of this in mind, the following extra-strength prosperity spell works by shifting your perspective and vibrational set point from one of fear and lack into one of love and gratitude. By concentrating on your generosity and sending it out in all directions like an expansive fountain of love, you activate the generosity of the God/Goddess/Universe, who multiplies the positivity you have launched and sends it back to you in a Niagara-sized waterfall of blessings and wealth.

A WEALTH ACTIVATION RITUAL

Ingredients

> 14 one-dollar bills that have been cleansed in sunlight (expose each side for five minutes)
>
> A clean glass bottle or jar of clear water with lid
>
> An empty glass Mason jar with lid

Essential oil of peppermint, spearmint, or eucalyptus (or incense with holder)

3 votive candles and holders: one blue, one green, and one white

Matches or lighter

On the morning or evening of a new moon, arrange the three candles on your altar or a clear, flat surface. Place the empty jar and the water behind them. Sit or stand in front of the candles with your spine straight. Close your eyes, take some deep breaths, and consciously relax your body. As a preliminary preparation, call on a helper or helpers of your choice (such as Archangel Michael or the God and Goddess) to vacuum away all negativity and stuck energy around you, and to surround you and your magical workspace in a sphere of bright white light in which only love remains and through which only love may enter.

Light the blue candle and say, "The planet prospers." Light the green candle and say, "My fellow humans prosper." Light the white candle and say, "I prosper."

Anoint one of the dollar bills with the oil as you inwardly bless and give thanks for the wealth you already have. (If your skin is extremely sensitive to oils, light a stick of mint or eucalyptus incense and waft the smoke around the dollar.) Then place it between your two palms so that your hands are in prayer pose.

With your hands still in prayer pose, rest your thumbs against your forehead. Conjure up all your most positive wishes for the entire planet. Visualize great abundance and blessings for all plants, animals, and people. See the rivers filled with clear, rushing water. Envision healthy and happy animals and vibrant, lush forests. Feel that everything is in harmony, in a mutually beneficial symbiosis. Send the energy of sustainable prosperity everywhere like flowing, sparkling blue light.

Now move your hands, still in prayer pose, until your thumbs are resting against your sternum. From your heart center and on the wings of love, send well wishes to all your fellow humans. Wish for and visualize continued abundance for all people: young, old, middle-aged, wealthy, poor, and middle class. See people of every nationality and on every continent smiling and happy, giving what they can and receiving what they need, with plenty of money and resources to spare and share. Send this loving energy to the hearts of all humans like flowing emerald green light.

Place your hands now, still in prayer pose, so that your thumbs are resting against your lower belly. Now remind yourself that "everyone deserves abundance, including me" and also "I am now willing to receive the abundant wealth that the universe desires to continually bestow upon me." Knowing that you are a beloved child of the God/Goddess/Universe, accept and acknowledge that receiving a generous flow of wealth and resources is your divine right and natural state. With the same love and compassion that you wish for others to thrive, wish and visualize this for yourself. See and feel yourself bathed in the glorious, infinite white light of abundance that moves through you continually like a fountain. Draw this cool, flowing, bubbling light up from a deep, endless well within the earth; also draw it down like a funnel from a cache of endless light above the earth's atmosphere, high above you in the cosmos. Know that doors of opportunity and luck are now energetically opening for you everywhere. Be willing to receive these blessings.

When this feels complete, say, "Thank you, thank you, thank you. Blessed be. And so it is." Then place the dollar into the empty jar.

Repeat this process every day until the full moon. Then, on the day of the full moon, with great love and generosity, and with great confidence in your own abundance, donate the $14 to a charity of your choosing. You can send it in the mail anonymously, place it in a donation jar at a business, or deliver it to the charity personally. Also on the day of the full moon, release the water into a body of water such as a lake, stream, or ocean. (If you're in a dry area or city, you might release it into a public water feature such as a fountain.) With each of these actions, understand that by contributing energy to the universal flow in the form of intentions and resources, you are tapping into your natural, endless flow of wealth.

Then, as with any wealth/prosperity ritual, follow your intuition and the natural flow of your joy when it comes to taking action in the physical world. This is not to say that unexpected windfalls won't fall in your lap, it's just to say that this will be exponentially less likely to occur if you are not simultaneously taking concrete, proactive steps toward improving your financial situation.

Advanced Prosperity Spell—Ellen

Prosperity spells are a type of magick that all of us find ourselves needing from time to time. No matter who you are, we all desire to feel prosperous and successful. Whether you are trying to catch up on the bills, saving for a better car or a home, or dealing with an unexpected expense does not matter. At the end of the day, we all need to cover our expenses and plan for the future.

Prosperity magick can be tricky. After researching the topic in depth a few years ago and writing a book on the subject, I have to admit that this type of magick is more complex and advanced than most folks realize. In truth, for effective prosperity magick, it all comes down to your mood and the state of mind that you are in when you cast any spells calling for healthy abundance and prosperity.

The following spell relies heavily on props and accessories, the idea behind this being that the more items you have in sympathy (that are associated or correspond with your magickal intention), the more focused you will be while casting the spell. This, then, will allow for truer and more robust magickal results.

Timing

Work this particular spell during a waxing moon for increase (the waxing moon is anytime between when the moon is in its new and full phases).

Work this spell on a Thursday (Jupiter's day) for prosperity or a Sunday (the sun's day) for success and riches. Timing is very important. Check your astrological calendar, and time this spell correctly. The waxing lunar phase and your chosen coordinating day of the week will add extra punch and power to the spellwork.

Supplies

> a green or gold votive or taper candle (to draw wealth, success, and prosperity)—use a gold candle if you cast on a Sunday and a green candle if you cast on a Thursday
>
> a coordinating candleholder
>
> a pair of lodestones (to attract wealth)

- golden magnetic sand (to draw prosperity to you)
- the Ace of Pentacles from a tarot deck (my *Witches Tarot* deck shows blooming honeysuckle on this particular card)
- lighter or matches
- a safe, flat work surface away from curious pets or small children
- Also choose one or all three of the following prosperity-associated herbs:
  High John the Conqueror root: the classic herbal accessory for prosperity magick
  Mint: an herb associated with wealth and riches
  Honeysuckle: this blooming vine is an herb associated with money and prosperity

Directions

Arrange the candle in its holder. Pour a thin line of magnetic sand in a circle around the candleholder. Note: Magnetic sand is super fine and can be messy should curious cats decide to explore your altar while your spell is working. So if you would prefer, sprinkle the magnetic sand in the bottom of your candleholder.

Arrange your lodestones, chosen herbs, and the Ace of Pentacles card in a manner you find pleasing around the candle. Take a moment to ground and center. Put your mind in a proper mood; focus on prosperity and how you will be successful. Do not focus on want or need—trust me. Keep your emotions upbeat, and your prosperity magick will flourish!

Then, when you are focused and calm, light the spell candle and repeat the following verse:

Green candle that burns with its flame so bright,
I call for prosperity on this night.
By the power in these stones, send abundance true,
May these herbs grant good fortune in all that I do.
The Ace of Pentacles shall be for me
A sign of abundant prosperity.
Now golden sand and lodestones draw money straight to me,
For the good of all, as I will it, so mote it be!

Allow the candle to burn out in a safe place on its own. You can leave the herbs and tarot card in place for a few days, so long as they are safe from little hands and curious paws.

For more spells, charms, and information on the topic of prosperity magick, please refer to my book *Practical Prosperity Magick*.

Protection Spells

Protection Prerequisites—Tess

Effective spiritual and energetic protection begins with a state of mind. And, like exercising or cultivating an artistic skill, this increases in depth and effectiveness over time with vigilant, regular upkeep. (I call it "magical hygiene.") So before we get to the spells, let's look at some of the positive habits that can contribute to experiencing reliable, lasting psychic protection on a daily basis.

Confidence

When I was a kid, someone (I don't remember who) told me that if I ever felt afraid while out in the world, I should not cower or tiptoe but walk like I was the most confident person in the world. This way, I would be less likely to attract predatory behavior because I would not be behaving like prey. What this person didn't tell me, but what I learned on my own, was that faking it actually helps you make it: when you move like you're confident, your brain believes that you are confident, and then—guess what? You *are* confident. (Or at least you're more so than you were before.)

Similarly, when you feel fearful, it's important to transform the inner fearful conditions into inner confident ones ASAP. This is because fear vibrates at a level that is more open to negativity and is not protective. Now, this might seem like a little mind trap or a slippery slope; after all, if you're already afraid, won't knowing this make you even more afraid? Perhaps, but *not if you remember to stop the cycle by immediately enlisting divine help.* To do this, you might call on Archangel Michael or the goddess Kali or whatever divine being or name feels most protective and effective for you. Then, once you ask for help (inwardly or aloud), know in your heart—or at least behave as if you know in your heart (faking it helps you make it, remember?)—that your help has arrived and that it's already begun to protect you in a most powerful and potent way. For example, if I'm walking in a scary alley, I might call on angelic bodyguards to flank me on all sides; then I'll continue walking with utter faith in their competence. Or if I feel myself slipping into a sketchy and anxious mindset, I'll replace my fearful monologue with an angelic invocation and visualization for as long as it takes to reprogram my pattern and feel my confidence return.

Grounding

Another prerequisite to holistic protection is grounding: connecting your personal energy with the energy at the core of the earth. This helps you feel anchored in a power that is greater than that within your little human energy field and aligns you with a greater and more expansive wisdom. I find that I feel best when I ground my energy daily as a part of my morning meditation, and I refresh my grounding anytime I begin to feel scattered, fearful, or spacey.

You may have already found your favorite way to ground your energy, but in case you haven't, my favorite is relaxing my body, with my spine straight, and sending roots of light deep into the core of the earth, then drawing golden-white earth light up from the core and into my root chakra. Then I see and feel this light moving up through my chakras and out through the crown of my head. Sometimes I reach branches high into the sky and bring cosmic light down from above, and other times I let my branches kiss the sky and then curl down back to earth like a weeping willow. Other methods include sending a "pranic tube" of light down into the earth to draw up the earth energy or sending a golden anchor deep down into the core of the earth in order to connect yourself to the core like a plug connects with an outlet.

Clearing and Shielding

The final protection prerequisite is a daily clearing and shielding. You can do this as part of a morning meditation and anytime you'd like an extra boost of protection. Clearing is important because like attracts like: if your energy is not clear and positive, it will be more likely to attract energy that is *not* clear and positive. Shielding is especially important for sensitive people because it helps us to refrain from picking up any energetic patterns that are from people, events, and conditions that have nothing to do with us.

Perhaps the simplest way to clear and shield is to request divine assistance in a way that feels powerful for you, and then to request a divine clearing of your personal energy field. You might visualize a glowing vacuum tube of light moving through your body and the sphere of space around you, powerfully removing cords of attachment, stagnant energy, and the energy of fear. Then request and visualize a sphere of golden white light. Set the intention that within this light only love remains, and through this light only love may enter.

An Old-Fashioned Garlic Protection Spell

Once you've got all of the above things working on your behalf, if you still feel that you could use an extra dose of protection, I have personally always found that nothing protects as reliably or completely as good old-fashioned garlic.

For example, once you empower the garlic (whether it's a clove, a head, a wreath or other arrangement, powder, or a supplement) in bright sunlight for at least five minutes (or by candlelight or fire if it's nighttime or it's cloudy out and you're in a pinch), and infuse the garlic with your clear intention to protect you from all negativity and ill will, perform any of the following garlic protection practices according to your situation and desire.

> Carry a clove of garlic as a protection amulet (I like to wrap one in cloth and safety-pin it under the front of my bra).

Hang a garlic wreath or arrangement on your front door or in a central location in your home.

Sprinkle garlic powder across your threshold or around the perimeter of your lot.

Take garlic supplements or cut a clove of garlic into small pieces and swallow them one at a time like pills to strengthen your personal energy field and keep negativity at bay.

Add fresh garlic or garlic powder to food.

For extra-strength home protection, for each door to the outside, pierce a clove of garlic with two pins so that they are crossing each other, tie in a red cotton pouch with hemp twine, and hang on the outside of each door.

Big Guns Protection Spell—Ellen

When it comes to protection magick, there are some days when a Witch has to call in the big guns. When would such a spell be necessary? Well, I hope you never find yourself in any of the following situations, but these are examples of what would make me call in the big guns: if your property had been vandalized or your car broken into; if you (or your loved ones) have a creeper or a stalker or, heaven forbid, were assaulted; if your home or business were robbed; if your reputation or honor has been called into question and it could affect your job and your children, and *you are innocent of any wrongdoing,* then here you go.

First things first. If you are the victim of a crime, then contact the authorities and get the wheels rolling on the mundane level. Report the crime, file a restraining order, and do whatever you have to do. Magick should work hand in hand with the mundane world.

Furthermore, I must caution you that this is not the spell for when you have had a bad day at work dealing with office politics. If you had an argument with someone and they turned things around on you, and then made you seem like the villain, this is not the spell for you. (Hint: If those last two examples happened, then you need to work on communication magick, *not* protection magick.) The following is the type of spell that you save for a disaster and hope you will never have to use it.

I will warn you again that, should you try working this spell when you yourself are the instigator—if you are doing anything illegal, morally unethical, or acting in a dishonorable fashion—then this magick will rebound right onto you. Protection magick can be tricky, and—juast as with any other magick—you must have your emotions in check and yourself under control. Otherwise, all you will do is breed chaos and cause even more problems. After all having a tantrum and throwing magick around only causes more turmoil. What you need to do is stand tall, calmly defend yourself, and work magick for a resolution.

Look at the words in this spell. You are basically asking the dark goddess to assist the miscreant to "fall by their own hand"—in other words, that their own behavior and actions will trip them up and tip off the authorities. This is the dark-goddess-will-make-sure-that-karma-will-find-you type of working. Also, you do not have to name the criminal, especially if you are not sure who they are. Just leave that to the dark goddess. Trust me, she can find them.

Timing

Work this particular spell during the last of the waning moon phase (those final days before the new moon, when the moon is barely visible in the sky).

Work this spell at sunset on a Saturday (Saturn's day). This is very important. Check your astrological calendar and time it correctly. This specific lunar phase, day of the week, and time of day will help to banish any obstacles to the criminal being caught. Consider that this is both the close of the week and the end of the daylight hours; that is a powerful combination.

Supplies

> a black votive or taper candle (to banish negativity and remove any emotional hold they or the event may have on you)
>
> a coordinating candleholder
>
> lighter or matches
>
> an item in sympathy with the event (for example, if your car or house was vandalized or robbed, then a photo of your house or car, a copy of the police report, and so forth)

a safe, flat work surface

Spell

Enemy mine, you have been warned: turn back from this path
Or you'll face my magick and the dark goddess's wrath.
The dark goddess protects me in my hour of need,
For I shall always defend me and mine if needs be.
Your power over me fades as this candle burns away,
By your own actions you'll be caught, and justice will hold sway.
Any crimes and misdeeds against me/us will now come to light
As I work this protection spell on the darkest of nights.
By all the power of three times three,
As I will it, then so shall it be!

Allow the candle to burn out in a safe place on its own. When the new waxing crescent appears in the western sky at sunset in a few days, begin work for healing and strength.

For more information on the topic of protection magick, please refer to my book *Practical Protection Magick*.

Love Spells

An Attraction Ritual—Tess

Many people are initially attracted to practicing magick because they want to do a love spell. When we're rookies, most of us have a romanticized, cinematic idea of how love spells will work: we'll drink the potion and everyone will love us, or we'll put powdered magnolia blossoms in someone's shoes and then he'll be perfectly faithful for the remainder of his days, or (who knows!) our perfect partner might even materialize before our eyes in a puff of rose-scented smoke.

And then, of course, we become more seasoned, and we realize that, in fact, it's a bit more complex than that. There are unmistakable underlying principles that dictate how our results will play out. Once we become aware of these principles, a lot of the magick works itself before we even crack a spell book or light a single candle. Not only that, but when we do decide to work a little love magic, we do it in a way that is exponentially wiser and more effective.

For example, below you'll find some of the main love magick principles I've noticed during my years of work in the field.

Like Attracts Like

If you're looking for a happy, stable, successful partner who has done a lot of inner work and is ready for a healthy, long-term relationship, or if you want your current partner to more closely resemble this description—and if these qualities don't even come close to describing you—sorry, honey, but it isn't going to happen. Until, of course, these qualities *do* describe you, in which case, sure! So get to work on cultivating these qualities within yourself. And if you'd like to attract a partner in the meantime, perhaps change your intention to attracting someone who is in a positive momentum and with whom you can harmoniously move toward these qualities together.

Similarly, if you do a lot of self-work and greatly improve your personal vibration, and the person that you are with does not have an interest in doing so, this relationship may naturally fall away so that you can attract someone who more closely matches you energetically.

Focus on You

Along the same lines, no matter what your intention when it comes to love magic, it's generally a good idea to focus on yourself rather than others. Of course you never, ever, *ever* want to do a love spell on someone else, as messing with someone else's free will will not result in a positive outcome for anyone, especially you. But because like attracts like (see above), if you cast a spell to make yourself attractive and magnetic, you will naturally attract and magnetize someone with similar qualities. Or, if you want to create relationship harmony, you might cast a spell to establish harmony within yourself.

Attract What You Need, not What (You Think) You Want

Magically attracting love is not like ordering takeout; it's much more mysterious. An ideal love match is one that continually challenges you, teaches you, opens your heart, and breaks down your defenses. In short, it might not actually look the way you think you want it to look. In fact, it probably won't. So, for example, if you do it right, a spell to attract your ideal partner will possibly result in attracting someone you didn't exactly expect.

All I'm saying here is to be open to that. We don't want you turning down the potential love of your life just because he doesn't, I don't know, teach yoga or look exactly like George Clooney.

Speaking of which, I don't recommend doing a love spell to attract a yoga teacher who looks like George Clooney. Don't limit the universe like that. Instead, you might do a love spell to attract your most ideal partner. Sure, add in a few deal breakers like someone with a positive mindset, healthy habits, and a career path that inspires him (or her), but let the universe surprise you when it comes to the minutiae. Like most magical intentions, love-related intentions are best when they're focused in their scope but not overly specific when it comes to the details.

Okay, now that you've been primed in some of the underlying mechanisms of love magic, on with the spell. This ritual works by making you so magnetic that you send smoke signals of irresistible attraction out into the ether. Expect plenty of interest and invitations in the days and weeks to follow.

Smoke Signal & Roses: An Attraction Ritual

Ingredients

>Petals from two red roses

>One red candle

>Other candles as necessary for a romantic ambiance

>Rosewater in a mister

>1 to 3 sticks of rose incense and incense holder

>Wine and chocolate (or another sensual snack such as strawberries)

On a Friday evening when the moon is between new and full, draw a warm bath. Add the rose petals from two red roses. Light a red candle and a stick of rose incense, then soak for at least twenty minutes. Ideally by candlelight, dry off and mist yourself with rosewater from head to toe, then smudge yourself with the rose incense. Now, still nude, move yourself and the incense to an area of your home where you can dance. (Light an additional stick of incense if necessary.) Light candles and play seductive music that makes your body want to move.

Say:

*I am divinely magnetic,
and I now attract a partner that is ideal for me in every way.*

Revel in the sensuality of the moment as you let your body dance slowly and hypnotically. Feel that the smoke from the incense is moving high into the sky, sending out your magnetic attractiveness in all directions. Make sure to light another stick if the first one burns all the way down and you still feel like dancing. When this feels complete, hold your hands up over your head and say:

*Thank you, thank you, thank you.
Blessed be. And so it is.*

Place your palms on the ground and send any excess energy you may have generated deep into the earth. Then turn the lights on, dress in evening wear that you feel great in, and have a glass of wine and some chocolate or another sensual treat.

Love Magick for a Family—Ellen

Love comes in a wondrous variety of forms. I thought it might be fun to do something a little different when it comes to love and spellwork. This spell was inspired by the illustration on the Ten of Pentacles card from my *Witches Tarot* deck. In my deck, this particular card shows a grandfather passing his magick to a new baby while the baby's parents look on from behind. A pretty house on the hill is in the background, and a loving, adorable dog sits by the grandfather's feet. This scene speaks of family strength, love, support, and of magickal legacies passed along to the next generation. It is a great focal point for this spell.

I have been asked many times how one builds a family legacy or tradition of magick. Well, the simple answer is that you live your magick every day, and you teach by example and share this spiritual lifestyle with your kids. My kids are all grown now, with homes and lives of their own. These days especially I see the influence that being raised by a Witch and a Witch-friendly father has had on them.

For example, it makes me proud that my oldest son put in a vegetable garden at his new house as soon as he could. Then he called his father and me to double check on the care of the lawn and the plants in the established garden that he inherited when he purchased the house. It warms my heart to know that all of my kids can identify plants, and each has a fine working knowledge of gardening from me and DIY experience, hunting, and fishing knowledge from their father.

Also, I find it sweetly amusing to have my sons and daughter whip out their own copies of my tarot deck and do a reading for themselves when they want to double check something—especially when they call to discuss their interpretation of the reading with me.

There is more to teaching your kids to appreciate the earth, Pagan values, and magick than just plopping a spell book down in front of them or dragging them off to yon local pride day. To be a good Pagan parent means you get involved with your kids. You love them, set boundaries, and teach them how to be exceptional people. As Witch and Pagan parents, we must realize that it is not just the spells we pass on; it's many other things as well.

Share with them things that many people have forgotten in this technology-driven age. Teach your kids how to hunt and fish. Get them involved in conservation and the care of the land. Teach them how to grow a garden and to raise flowers, herbs, and vegetables. Then go a step further and teach them how to cook. (Their future partner will thank you for that.) Do arts and crafts, home maintenance, repairs, and decorating projects together.

While you are spending quality time with them as they grow, also be sure to teach them to be open-minded, hard working, loyal, truthful, and kind. These qualities will be a great boon to them as they become adults and go out in the world to make their own home and eventually raise their own family someday. Sure, it's a lot of work, but it is also a lot of fun!

Here is a spell to reinforce your heritage and the magickal legacy that you are working towards building with the people you call family.

Timing

Work this particular spell during the waxing moon phase. As the moon increases, so will the bond of your family.

Opportune days of the week include Friday (love) and Wednesday (communication).

Supplies

A brown votive or taper candle (to represent hearth and home)

A coordinating candleholder

Lighter or matches

Ten of Pentacles tarot card

A photo or photos of your family

A safe, flat work surface

Directions

Set up the candle in its holder and arrange the photo/s of your family and the Ten of Pentacles tarot card on either side of the candle. Take a moment to ground and center. As you do, focus on happy memories and your family's loving bond. When you are ready, light the candle and repeat the following spell verse:

Love of our family and home is strong and true,
May the gods watch over us in all that we do.
By the powers of earth, air, fire, and water,
Our legacies are taught by mother to daughter
Strengthened by every passing dusk and dawn,
Heritage is passed on from father to son.
Ten pentacles to show a wealth of love,
May we all be blessed by the gods above.

Allow the candle to burn out in a safe place. Keep the photo/s and the tarot card together until the day after the full moon to help reinforce the magick. If you like, this spell verse also makes for a nice magickal prayer. Blessed be to you and yours!

Glamour Spells

Fun with Glamoury—Tess

Glamoury is a way of casting an aura within and around oneself in order to make one's presence felt and perceived in a specific way. This type of magick is usually practiced for the purpose of affecting others in ways that help to draw a desired quality or condition such as influence, authority, or success in a particular endeavor. While at first glance this might sound like a way of manipulating others and overriding their free will, when done correctly, it actually isn't. Rather, while others may react differently because of your magical efforts, glamour spells focus on creating changes within and around *you*. You might think of it as an invisible, energetic costume or accessory that you're wearing. So just as wearing a sexy dress would not be seen as affecting someone else's free will but rather as a personal choice that will affect the way you are perceived in a particular way, glamoury wouldn't either. In other words, while you *are* creating changes to your own personal energy in the hopes that others will react in a certain way, the way they *actually* react is still up to them.

All that being said, sometimes you might like to cast a glamour spell just for fun. After all, what Witch doesn't like to have a little fun with her magical abilities every now and then?

The two glamour spells below will give you a couple of options for various moods and intentions.

ACORN AURA OF SUCCESS CHARM

Supplies

> A necklace or bracelet with an acorn charm
>
> A bundle of dried white sage
>
> A large red candle
>
> A stick of cinnamon incense with holder

You know those people who just seem to ooze the energy of success? Those charismatic men and women who waltz into a room and everyone starts trying to hire them or impress them or just figure out their secret? Because naturally, just like the old saying "the rich get richer," success—or even just an aura of success—

draws more success. Perform this ritual once, and you'll have a success charm for a lifetime. Just wear it anytime you'd like to *be* that person who dances through the world, attracting more and more of the dazzling success that it seems like she already has.

First, take your time and acquire an attractive necklace or bracelet that features a single charm that resembles an acorn: a symbol of great luck, power, and promise. You might check etsy.com or, if you're crafty, you can make it yourself. Wait until you find or make something that feels really right to you for the purpose.

Next, on the day of the full moon (or a day or two before), safely bathe your jewelry in white sage smoke for at least two minutes, and then place it on a white cloth in bright sunlight for at least five minutes. That evening, as the moon is bright in the sky, light a large red candle and a stick of cinnamon incense on your altar or a flat surface.

Holding the necklace in your right palm, face east. Say, "I call on Archangel Raphael and the element of air."

Face south and say, "I call on Archangel Michael and the element of fire."

Face west and say, "I call on Archangel Gabriel and the element of water."

Face north and say, "I call on Archangel Uriel and the element of earth."

Face the candle and incense and say, "I call on Archangel Metatron and the element of spirit."

Now hold the jewelry in your open right palm, cupping your left palm beneath it. Say the following:

By the power of earth, air, fire, and water,
By the power of the archangels,
I now bless this charm with the energy of success.
When I wear it, I feel success.
When I wear it, I attract success.
When I wear it, I am Success personified.
All doors open for me.
All opportunities are irresistibly magnetized to me.
I am blessed with luck and prosperity beyond my fondest imaginings.
Thank you, thank you, thank you. Blessed be. And so it is.

Visualize yourself being cloaked in a bright, sunny sphere of successful light whenever you wear the charm. Then place the charm on your neck or wrist.

Now face north and say, "Uriel and the element of earth, I thank you."

Face west and say, "Gabriel and the element of water, I thank you."

Face south and say, "Michael and the element of fire, I thank you."

Face east and say, "Raphael and the element of air, I thank you."

Face the candle and say, "Metatron and the element of spirit, I thank you."

Extinguish the candle and let the incense continue to burn all the way down. Save the charm to wear on those days that you need an extra kick of luck and success. (If you wear it constantly it will lose its potency over time, but if you save it for special days you will recharge it every time you wear it.)

ROSE WATER AND WITCH HAZEL YOU-CAN'T-RESIST MIST

Ingredients

    An image of Venus or Aphrodite

    A mister of rosewater

A splash of witch hazel extract

A small moonstone

A pink candle

A stick of vanilla incense and holder

This mist potion will cloak you in a glamour of irresistibility, pure and simple. This can come in handy for a number of reasons, among them seduction, beauty, and influence.

On a Friday when the moon is between new and full, place an image of Venus or Aphrodite on your altar or another flat surface, along with a pink candle and a stick of vanilla incense. Light the candle and incense and call on the goddess of love. Bathe the moonstone in the incense smoke and mentally infuse it with the energy of charm and irresistibility. See this energy as white light containing pale pink sparkles. When this feels complete, place it in the mister of rose water. Add a splash of witch hazel, close the mister, and shake.

While holding it in both hands, visualize this white light with pale pink sparkles coming down from above, entering the crown of your head, moving into your heart, down your arms, and into the liquid. See and feel the liquid pulsating with this light.

Say, "When I'm cloaked in this mist, no one can resist."

Then spray yourself and your aura generously with the mist. Thank the goddess of love, set the mister by the candle and incense, and allow the incense to burn all the way down; then extinguish the candle. Generously mist yourself before any occasion when you want to turn on the charm.

The Magick of Blending In—Ellen

A glamourie is the purposeful change of your appearance on both a physical and metaphysical level by the use of magick. When cast correctly, it is powerful magick indeed, as it gives the caster an advantage over a situation or another person, which is why some folks consider them to be unethical. Personally, I believe that a glamour-type of spell would fall in the area of grey magick. Glamouries—like any other magick—are neutral. Honestly, it all boils down to how you cast them. If you are casting a glamour on *yourself* to smooth your way or bring peace to a tough situation, then that is a very clever bit of magick indeed. Every once in a while you can find yourself in a situation where people do not react well once they realize you are a Witch. It may be the area in which you live or it may be a circumstance where you simply do not fit their idea of what a Witch is, and that blows their mind. So they get nervous, suspicious, and then hostile.

I have been out in the open about my practice for twenty years, and as a well-known Witch I really had not experienced any serious problems because of my beliefs in quite some time. Then a family member ended up in the hospital for several days, and I watched with surprise, then consternation, at the reactions and questions my family member received about me—first with the medical staff at the hospital, then at the new doctor's office for follow-up visits. During this time I had also started to see a new doctor, and people reacted in various degrees to the fact that the nice middle-aged lady who seemed pretty normal was, in fact, wearing a pentagram. It was an eye opener.

I admit, it took me a bit to figure out what was going on. I try to be friendly and polite to everybody, and it was concerning to see people recoil, become afraid, act suspicious, or become openly hostile to my presence. Sometimes people's reactions were comical, like a sitcom overreaction of their own nervousness, and other times it was really bad, and I was confronted with out-and-out hostility and anger.

It made me sit down and ask myself what my best course of action would be. I realized that it was the fact that the confident, nicely dressed, normal-looking lady with successful adult kids was openly wearing a small silver pentagram that caused such severe reactions with new people I encountered. I was the last thing they expected. Sure, if I were some emo kid running around all dressed in black, nobody would flinch. But a seemingly typical fifty-year-old woman they could not handle. After so many years of being open about my faith and being a known author on Witchcraft with no negative reactions, the climate in my part of the country had suddenly changed.

Over the years, folks had often asked me if I had problems being a well-known Witch while living in the Midwest. My answer had always been no. Now, suddenly, I discovered firsthand how many other

Witches and Pagans across the country were treated if they were open about their faith. And like it or not, I needed to reasses and make some changes unless I wanted to keep dealing with more hostility.

So I tackled the problem like the practical Witch that I am. I decided to start by making an effort to blend in a bit more while I was out in public or in any new mundane environment. For example, I toned down the magickal jewelry. I made a real effort to not wear so many black clothes. (Show me a Witch who doesn't have a closet full of black clothing!) I compromised and added more colorful accessories to my midnight-colored wardrobe: jewel tones and pops of bright colors worked well with the black pieces of clothing that I had, and it did help. Changing out some accessories and jewelry began to work really quickly—the magick of fashion at its best! I also made a promise to myself to not let this experience sour me, and I tried to keep a sense of humor and just go about my business the best I could.

Also, on the morning after a full moon before the moon set—while both the moon and the sun were in the sky—I worked a glamour to soften people's negative reactions to me and smooth my way around new mundane people in present and future everyday situations.

Here is a spell that calls on the constantly changing energy of the moon. This is a glamour-type of color magick that will help you blend in and go unnoticed in sticky situations. Work this spell the morning after a full moon. If things are especially intense, then I suggest wearing lunar-associated colors such as silver, soft grey, white, and the palest blues, or just add some jewel tones or pops of bright colors to your witchy black wardrobe. Before you head out for the day, enchant your outfit so you can go about your business quietly, without a fuss.

This spell helps to smooth out obstacles that are in your way. It also encourages people to react to you in a more positive way and calm frayed tempers. Once you are dressed and ready to go, stand in front of a mirror, look yourself in the eye, and then cast the glamour on yourself.

The lunar shades of magick are white, blue, and silvery,
Concealment and illusion they'll grant softly to me.
There will be soft light and harmony all around me,
I'll move through the shadows, embracing the glamoury.
A touch of color on witchy black creates a bit of pop,
All unkind and negative reactions to me now will stop.
Now smooth all obstacles that are in my way,
Peace and quiet are the order of the day.
By the power of color, this glamour is cast,
Swirl around me now and make the magick last.

Now go about your day and be at peace. Blessed be.

Banishing Spells

Banishing Unwanted Patterns with the Akashic Field—Tess

Everything is energy. You might think of your life as a song or a geometrical pattern—a distinctive swirl of energy. Not only does the song or pattern that is you contain a bunch of smaller and more intricate songs and patterns, but it is also a component of the even larger song or pattern that is everything. When we banish, what we are essentially doing is reaching into the energetic reality and pulling out a particular pattern that we no longer desire. It's like removing a certain melody from a musical songbook or unraveling a certain motif from a tapestry.

The famed psychic Edgar Cayce—and, more recently, the philosopher and integral theorist Ervin Laszlo—referred to the underlying energetic reality as the Akashic Field and the patterns that define one's life experience as his or her Akashic Record. Consequently, these terms have become quite popular in New Age circles.

And since I often like to throw some of my New Agey sensibilities into my magical mix, the following ritual draws upon the awareness of the Akashic Field in order to banish old patterns for good. It works by first clearing these patterns, then rewriting them. I've found it to be extremely powerful.

AKASHIC RECORD REWRITE RITUAL

Ingredients

Notebook

Pen

White candle on plate

Sea salt

Frankincense or cedar incense and holder

Lighter

This ritual is good to perform anytime you notice a pattern in your life that you'd like to remove. For example, this pattern may be a challenge such as a fender bender, a health condition, or a financial situation that seems to recur in a number of guises and incarnations, a harmful habit such as smoking or drinking, or even an ongoing relationship with someone whom you know you'd prefer not to see anymore but for whatever reason haven't been able to kick out the door.

First, notice the pattern and write it down in a journal or notebook, using a word or short phrase. For example, you might write something like:

Car troubles
Weakened immune system
Financial worries
Smoking habit
Alcoholism
Relationship with _____.

Once you've done this, set a white candle on a plate, surround it with a ring of sea salt, and place it on your altar. Light the candle along with a stick of frankincense or cedar incense. Call on Archangel Metatron, who is one of the keepers of the Akashic Records, to assist you in this banishment.

Sit comfortably in front of your altar. Take some deep breaths and consciously relax every muscle in your body. When you feel relaxed and centered, gaze at your notebook and consider what you've written down. Now ask yourself: is there a fear that I associate with this pattern? If so, what is it? Write it down. For example, you might write something like:

Fear of strength
Fear of weakness
Fear of poverty
Fear of success
Fear of loneliness

For whatever you wrote down, now write down a word that is the opposite and that feels very empowering and positive for you. For each of the following, for example, you might write a dash and then write:

Comfort with strength
Strength
Wealth
Comfort with success
Loving support

Now ask yourself: is there a belief that might be underlying this pattern? If so, what is it? Again, write it down. It might be something like:

I am unsafe.

I am unworthy.

If I speak my truth, no one will like me.

If I only hang out with emotionally healthy people, no one will need me.

Consider a new, more empowering belief that you'd like to replace this one with. For the above, you might write:

I am safe.

I am worthy.

When I speak my truth, I love myself. When I love myself, I attract love.

I love being in relationships with emotionally healthy people, and I feel treasured and respected by them in the most positive of ways.

Please note: it's a good idea to be open to your fear and your belief possibly not making obvious sense, at least at first. Really take your time and find what feels true to you and what resonates with your soul.

Now you're going to write a banishment script and a script to rewrite the Akashic Records. It's going to go like this:

With the help of my divine self and Archangel Metatron, I now choose to release the pattern of [first thing you wrote] from my Akashic Records. I now release it in all directions of time and all dimensions of reality. I now cancel, clear, and delete it so that it is no longer present in any capacity.

I now choose to release the fear of [second thing you wrote] from my Akashic Records. I release it in all directions of time and all dimensions of reality. I now cancel, clear, and delete it so that it is no longer present in any capacity. I now rewrite it with the energy of [third thing you wrote], which is now present in all directions of time and all dimensions of reality.

I now choose to release the belief of [fourth thing you wrote] from my Akashic Records. I release it in all directions of time and all dimensions of reality. I now cancel, clear, and delete it so that it is no longer present in any capacity. I now rewrite it with the belief of [fifth thing you wrote], which is now present in all directions of time and all dimensions of reality.

Thank you, thank you, thank you. Blessed be. And so it is.

Now that you've written your script, relax again and take three deep breaths. Then tap your thymus (located at your upper chest, halfway between the center of your sternum and the center of your throat) lightly with your right hand as you powerfully and purposefully recite the script that you just wrote.

Finish by thanking Archangel Metatron and thanking yourself. Allow the candle to continue to burn at least until the incense burns all the way down. Then flush the salt down the toilet and wash the plate thoroughly. (It's okay to use the candle again in the future.)

A quick caveat: be ready for things to shift. Working on such a deep level might cause things to seem a little chaotic at first as your life becomes accustomed to the new patterns, but hang in there— you'll experience desirable results.

Saturn's Day Banishing Spell—Ellen

Banishing spells are tricky little buggers—not because they are difficult to perform but because, honestly, it is hard to tell whether you need to work one or not. In my opinion, a banishing spell is more effective than, say, a binding spell. Why? Because with a binding spell you often inadvertently end up binding the problem person or negative situation even closer to you! When you work a binding spell, you need to be extremely careful with your phrasing. This is why I prefer banishing spells.

A banishing spell is best performed when there is an energy or situation that needs to be removed from your life. How will you know when you need to perform a banishing? If you feel anxious for no real reason, when things feel magickally "off," or you feel that you are being worn down by negativity in your own home. And if you are concerned that you may be the target of negative emotions such as jealousy or anger from another, it's time to work a banishing.

Banishings are best performed in your own home because…wait for it…this is where you live, sleep, love, work your magick, and (hopefully) relax. Your home is probably the spot where your magickal power is the most centered. Since it is the place where you relax and sleep on a regular basis, it is often the place where you can be the most vulnerable magickally, for the simple reason that when you are home, you feel that you can be yourself and feel safe. So this is where you should target your efforts to banish unwanted energies and spells.

Also, I would like you to consider that if you are experiencing energetic problems in your home, it could be lingering magick of *your own* that is floating around and not the attacking energies of another. Stray bits of your own magick can build up over time in your home and cause chaos, especially if you do not purposefully clear it out on a regular basis.

Let's clean house! If you ever have wondered what you would use a ritual broom for, then this is your answer. To start the process of this banishing spell, take a critical look at your home. Seriously, look at your corners, and get rid of any cobwebs, dust, and dirt! This *is* the perfect way to banish negativity and clean up any stray vibes from old spells. Remove all junk and clutter that has accumulated. Recycle what you can, and donate unused items to charity. Clean everything. We are talking hardcore cleaning here, folks. Scrub, mop, dust, sweep, and vacuum. Clean out the closets, wash the windows, change the sheets on the bed, and again: remove clutter! Clutter, dust, and dirt hold onto negative emotions and stagnant energy. Get them out of your house!

To make the big energetic cleanup a magickal act, employ some magickal timing. For best results, I suggest working this on a Saturday, either at sunset or in a waning moon phase. By timing your work when you have the decreasing energies of a waning moon, the closing energies of the end of the day (sunset), and the final day of the week, you are working things to your own advantage. Plus, there are the planetary energies of Saturn, which include karma and banishing to work with.

Saturn's Day Banishing Spell

To begin, I suggest burning your favorite cleansing incense (sandalwood is a good choice) while you physically dust, sweep, vacuum, and pick up. Be ruthless! And do not let boxes full of items you no longer use sit by your front door, either! Load them up in the car and move them out.

Once you have your home cleared of junk and clutter, and when everything is all cleaned and sparkling, then light a white votive candle and place it in a holder. Place it in the center of your home. Hold your hands up and on either side of the candle flame. Visualize that the light from the flame illuminates your very core. Now repeat the following spell verse:

By the power of Saturn's day and the closing week,
All negative energy and bad vibes now must leave.
My magickal home is now clean, cleared, and refreshed,
So this new magick can come in and work with zest!
Depart, old spells and stray, worn-out charms,
Now dissolve benignly and cause no harm.
This spell candle will draw in all negativity,
Like a moth to a flame, to be burned off completely
By all the power of hearth and home,
This house is cleared as my charm is sung!

Take your ritual or household broom and seal this spell by ritually sweeping the main thresholds clean. The threshold is any main entrance into your home; you probably have more than one. For example, in my home there is the front door, the back door, and the garage door. Go to the thresholds one at a time and make three big sweeps with your broom across the threshold. As you do, say these lines:

A sweep for the Maiden, the Mother, and the Crone,
Triple Goddess, seal this spell and protect my home.

Repeat these two lines at each threshold. Then go back to where the candle is burning, and ground and center. After you have finished, put your broom away. Move the white votive spell candle and incense (if you have any still burning) to a safe place, and let them burn out. Votive candles can take six to eight hours to burn out. It's important to let this particular candle burn out until it is gone. Look at the spell verse—you announced that as it burns away, the candle will draw negativity straight into it and remove it, or burn it off.

Wash the votive cup with salted water after the candle is gone. Announce over the now clean and empty votive cup, "By salt and water, this vessel is cleansed of all negativity and leftover magick." Put the clean votive candle cup away. Finally, to keep the energies of your home on track, I would perform a big cleansing once a month. Try this just once, and you will be a believer.

Full Moon Rituals

Basic Full Moon Ritual—Tess

While each phase of the moon possesses its own vital magical qualities, when the moon is full, magical energies are at a peak. Intentions set into motion since the most recent new moon gain energetic momentum, and our metaphysical work is amplified and intensified. As such, rituals performed when the full moon appears in the sky just feel right. Consciously experiencing the energetic fullness that characterizes this time and then releasing this energy with positive, focused intent allows you to ride the natural tide of energy. This not only lets a Witch nourish her goals, desires, and the most positive conditions of her life with a burst of magical energy, but it also helps reduce her everyday anxiety and stress by relieving the buildup of energy that naturally accumulates around magically sensitive people as the moon waxes to full.

While no two full moon rituals of mine have ever been exactly alike (because of various intentions, moods, astrological factors, etc.), below you'll find a sample solitary ritual. Feel free to adapt or riff on it according to your desires.

BASIC FULL MOON RITUAL

Ingredients

    2 tablespoons sea salt

    A sprig of rosemary

    A white rose

    Frankincense or nag champa incense and holder

    Small sage bundle (with jar and lid)

    White candle and holder

    Notebook or paper

    Pen

In the evening when you won't be disturbed, draw a warm bath to prepare yourself energetically and get into the magical mindset. Add 2 tablespoons of sea salt, a sprig of rosemary, and the petals of one white rose. Light a white candle and soak by candlelight for at least twenty minutes. (If you don't have a bathtub, just shower.) Dry off and dress in really luxurious and comfy clothes or eveningwear or go skyclad (nude).

Set a magical atmosphere by lighting candles on your altar and around the room, as well as a stick of frankincense or nag champa incense. Light a small bundle of dried white sage and smudge the room, then extinguish by sealing in a jar. You might also play relaxing, uplifting, or entrancing instrumental music.

Now, making sure to have your notebook, pen, candle, and lighter nearby, cast a circle around yourself. (If you're not familiar with this practice, simply stand in a central location with your wand or index finger extended as if you're pointing at the floor. Imagine a laser beam of highly protective white light extending out from the end of your wand or index finger, and draw a circle approximately 5 or 6 feet in diameter around yourself while slowly turning in a clockwise direction. When this is complete, feel and know that you are completely safe and protected within this circle. As a focusing aid before casting a circle, some people like to draw an actual circle with chalk or use a round rug or demarcate a circle with scarves or string.)

Standing in the center of the circle, face east. Say, "I call on the element of air." Feel a breeze whipping around your body and envision wind rushing through trees.

Face south. Say, "I call on the element of fire." Feel yourself being cleansed in a fiery inferno of light and envision crackling flames.

Face west. Say, "I call on the element of water." Feel a wave of cool ocean water rushing around you and envision roaring, frothy blue waves.

Face north. Say, "I call on the element of earth." Feel as if you're buried up to your neck in fragrant, moist, fertile soil. Inhale the scent and solidity of the earth as you allow your body to relax and be nourished.

Still facing north, say, "I call on the element of spirit." Feel/imagine/sense a column of vibrant white light completely encompassing you and your circle, connecting with the earth below, and reaching high up into the cosmos. See this pillar grow deep roots that connect you with the core of the earth, and see the top of this pillar go up and up, out of the earth's atmosphere, until it connects with the Infinite. Draw earth energy up and cosmic energy down to meet within your heart.

Now sit in the center of the circle facing any of the four cardinal directions (choose the direction that feels most powerful for you).

Light the candle. With notebook and pen in hand, make a list of all the things you'd like to nourish and bless in your life, as well as all the energies and conditions that you'd like to draw in. State the things you'd like to summon in the present tense, as if they're already true. For example, you might write:

I bless my relationship with _____.

I bless this home.

I bless my career.

I nourish my health.

I nourish my friendships.

I receive generous financial windfalls.

I receive wonderful opportunities from expected and unexpected sources.

I am totally open and receptive to all the love and abundance of the universe.

When this is complete, write: *Thank you, thank you, thank you. Blessed be. And so it is.* Then sign and date the paper.

Now read your list aloud, finishing with "Thank you, thank you, thank you. Blessed be. And so it is." Know that as you do so, the full moon and the elements fully support your intentions in all ways. Fold the paper into quarters, making sure to fold it toward yourself each time. Then place it under the lit candle. Sit for a moment basking in the confident inner knowing that your ritual has been a success.

Then, with the candle still lit, face west and say, "Element of water, you were here, and I thank you."

Face south and say, "Element of fire, you were here, and I thank you."

Face east and say, "Element of air, you were here, and I thank you."

Face north and say, "Element of earth, you were here, and I thank you."

Still facing north, say, "Element of spirit, you were here, and I thank you."

Hold your arms over your head as if opening up in wonder to the sky and say, "Thank you, thank you, thank you. Blessed be. And so it is."

To release the energy further, spin in a circle counterclockwise and then fling your arms up as if you're flinging rose petals to the sky.

Finally, earth the power by placing your palms on the floor or lying flat on your back, envisioning any excess energy you may still have in your aura dripping into the earth, leaving you with a perfectly balanced, harmonious, and grounded energetic field.

Full Moon Rededication Ritual—Ellen

At various points in our lives, we all need to refresh and reaffirm our initiatory vows as Witches, which is known as a rededication. Perhaps you have had a major change in your life: marriage, divorce, leaving a coven or finding a new one. Perhaps you finished school or started a new career. Maybe you moved to a new area or you just became a parent or you are now a crone or sage. The reasons for wanting to rededicate, reconnect, and to restate your vows are as numerous as the stars in the sky. It is not to be done lightly. I know some Witches who perform a rededication once a year, on the anniversary of their first initiation into the Craft. At the end of the day, realize that this is a personal decision; I think a private full moon ritual is just the ticket in which to do this.

Preparation

To begin, I would take a ritual bath or shower. Put on your ritual wear or clean clothes. Don't just schlepp around in your pajamas! Wear something nice, as if you were going on a date. If you can, and the temperature allows for it, go barefoot.

Timing

Perform this at moonrise on the night of a full moon. If weather permits, I would work this ritual outdoors or, if you must, stand by a window and allow the moon's light to wash over you and your work area.

Supplies

> A white votive or taper candle (white is an all-purpose color and a good choice for new beginnings)

A coordinating candleholder

A piece of tumbled moonstone

Fresh white roses, white lilies, or white carnations in a vase of clean water (see below for flower meanings)

Your favorite incense and a holder

Lighter or matches

An item in sympathy with the event: your special piece of magickal jewelry (we all have one) such as a ring, a significant necklace, or your pentagram pendant

A safe, flat work surface

A cup of juice or wine

Directions

As you set up your work area, take a few moments to ground and center. Arrange the candle, stone, incense holder, flowers, cup of wine/juice, and your jewelry in a manner you find pleasing. If you like, cover the altar with a pretty piece of cloth. Make this as simple or as elaborate as your personal taste dictates.

Now, take a good look at your rededication altar. You have all of four of the elements represented. The tumbled moonstone for earth, the (soon to be) candle flame for fire, the incense smoke for air, and the water in the flower vase for—well, water! The white flowers represent new beginnings and celebrations. If you chose carnations, they represent practicality, energy, and vitality. If you chose roses, you have added the energies of tradition, emotions, and love. If you chose lilies, then you have passion and enchantment added to your ritual. Once you are all set up, focus on why you are here and the reaffirmation to the gods and goddesses that you are about to undertake. Be joyful and reverent.

Light the incense and place it in the holder. Allow the scented smoke to waft over you and your work surface. Hold up the jewelry and allow it to be blessed by the incense smoke too. When finished, set your piece of jewelry back down next to the unlit candle. When you are ready to begin the rededication, light the candle and repeat the following spell verse:

Under an enchanted full moon of white,
I cast important magick here tonight.
I call on the earth, fire, water, and wind,
Let my Witch's lunar magick begin.
May the Old Ones bless my magickal path,
And bless me with a wisdom that will last.
To bring love, comfort, to protect and heal,
With these rhyming words, my vow will now seal.

Pick up your jewelry and hold it up to the light of the moon for a few moments. Now put it back on. Pick up your glass of juice or wine, toast the moon, and speak to the Old Ones in your own words. Relax and enjoy the moment and the magickal atmosphere that you have created. Now close the ritual with the following lines:

By all the powers of three times three,
As I will it, then so shall it be!

Pour a little of the juice or wine on the ground as an offering. Take one of the white flowers and leave it in the garden as an offering to the gods. Now you can sit under the moon and meditate if you choose. Take this opportunity to note this occasion down in your personal Book of Shadows. Note any dreams you have upon awakening the next morning; they may be especially significant.

Allow the candle to burn out in a safe place. If you need to move it inside where you can keep it attended, do so. If you had to work your ritual indoors, then pour a little bit of the wine or juice down the drain, where it will eventually make its way to the earth.

Clean up your supplies. Keep the moonstone with you as a token of your rededication. The rest of the fresh flowers should be displayed someplace prominent in your home until they begin to fade, then return them neatly to nature by recycling them with your yard waste or adding them to your compost. Wash the vase and save it for another time.

Enjoy the rest of your evening. Congratulations on your rededication, and blessed be!

"On the Fly" Spells

Four Fast Spells—Tess

Sometimes you're out in the world and something needs to be dealt with right away. You can't take the time to gather spell ingredients, take a bath, or even light a candle! Case in point: once Ellen and I were sharing a hotel room in Washington, DC, for an author event, and I realized that I had left my Kindle on the plane. When I started to go into loosely disguised panic mode, Ellen calmly taught me one of her favorite "find it" charms (see below). I promptly recited the words and did the visualization as per her instructions, and voila! Not only did I feel better right away, but after filing a lost and found report with the airline, within a week or two my Kindle arrived in my mailbox, safe and sound. (Thanks again, Ellen! And God/dess! And American Airlines!)

Here are some other useful, discreet little tricks you can store up your sleeve just in case you ever need them.

ELLEN'S FIND IT CHARM

Relax and strongly envision the object you desire to find. Imagine circling it in a silver cord and then tugging it toward you via the cord as you chant, "What was lost now is found as my magick circles round." Repeat two more times (for a total of three times), then relax in the confidence that the item is on its way back to you.

TRAFFIC CHARM

I've been living in—and navigating—Los Angeles for a good long percentage of my life now, and this little traffic trick is one of the lessons this city has motivated me to learn. Because let's face it: if you let it, traffic can pack a pretty negative punch. Not only can it make you late, it can also (perhaps more alarmingly) make you stressed! And what's worse for your health and the quality of your life than stress? Not much.

So here's what you do: you decide to love the traffic. You change your inner monologue from one of dismay and frustration to one of gratitude and love. Even if you feel like you're faking or forcing it at first, keep at it—because, after all, your frustration is not going to change the situation; it's only going to exacerbate your unpleasant experience. If you're going to be late, you're going to be late whether or not you berate the situation. Not only that, but a New Agey phrase that I have found to be quite accurate is *what we resist persists*. So when we take the resistance away and begin to honestly accept what's happening, the traffic congestion often seems to magically dissipate right along with your stressful thoughts about it.

To give you an example, this is how my inner monologue might go when I begin to work this little charm:

"Wow, the sunshine is so gorgeous reflecting off those windshields. This really is a pretty freeway, I'm so glad I get a chance to really soak it in. Look at that hawk! And those purple blossoms in the distance are just gorgeous. You know, my car is really great. I'm so lucky to have a car that runs so well. Oh, I love this song. And now I have time to actually listen to it intently! This is just getting better and better. I could honestly sit here all day."

It is hilarious how quickly traffic picks up once I really begin to get into the enjoyment of it all.

Turn Your Water into a Potion

If you wish you had a magick potion for any purpose at all, just send the vibration of your intention into the water, and guess what? You've got one. Homeopathic remedies such as flower and gem essences draw upon the principle that liquid stores vibration, and that imbibing that vibration can shift your personal energy in a subtle yet very powerful way. And just like flowers and gems, our thoughts, feelings, and intentions possess very distinct vibratory qualities.

So, let's say you'd like a potion to help you focus on a test. In this case, you might hold your water bottle or a glass of water in both hands and visualize very bright white light coming down from above, entering the crown of your head, and moving down to your heart and out through your hands, into the water. Then conjure up a feeling and sense of extreme mental clarity. In any way that feels powerful for you, ask the Divine to help you channel the energies and qualities of focus, attention, memory, and alertness into the water. Feel and sense your hands and the bottle pulsating intensely with this energy. Thank your divine helper and drink the water or sip it throughout the test.

DECIDE WHICH ITEM TO PURCHASE

Perhaps you're trying to decide whether to purchase the ginger tea or the peppermint tea, or maybe you're wondering whether you should go with the red shoes or the cheetah-print shoes. In either case, hold the first item in your hands. Relax, breathe, and notice your energy. How vibrant do you feel? How strong do you feel? How exhilarated and empowered do you feel? Then do the same with the second item. Which one gives you a greater sense of well-being? Which one sparks your inspiration and your joy more intensely? Obviously, that's the one.

Magick At Your Fingertips—Ellen

I love the idea of magick on the fly—spontaneous spells that require nothing but the sound of your voice, your knowledge, and, of course, your magickal intention to create a positive change. As Witches and magicians, we spend a lot of time discussing timing and lunar phases, but we are not always able to wait for the "perfect" moon phase or day of the week. Sometimes you have to take action right now!

So what is a Witch to do? Well, I have always felt it important to have a basic working knowledge of the days of the week and their magickal attributes. That way, you know what is in play energetically each and every day *and* you can then use this information to your benefit. One of the first lessons you probably learned as a Witch was that if the moon is waxing (from new to full), then you work for increase. On the other hand, if the moon is waning (the day after the full moon to the day of the new moon), then you should work to decrease.

For those of you who don't have your basics memorized, check out the following correspondences. Just memorize the basics, and you are good to go: day of the week and its magickal associations—*Sunday, Sun, success*, for example.

Keep it simple and make it fun! That way you will memorize it faster. So then, when it comes to making magick on the fly, having that basic knowledge memorized and at your fingertips can make the difference between your spells sputtering and stalling or really taking off and manifesting quickly!

DAILY MAGICKAL CORRESPONDENCES

Sunday: Sunday corresponds to the sun, our closest star. This day is for success, wealth, and fame. Sundays are for personal achievements of any kind such as working toward a promotion at your job, seeking fame and wealth, or being acknowledged for a job well done. Keywords: Sunday, Sun, success/wealth.

Monday: This day of the week is dedicated to the moon and all of her magick and mystery. Mondays are for women's mysteries, goddess magick, illusion, glamoury, prophetic dreaming, emotions, safe travel, and fertility. Keywords: Monday, moon, goddess/glamoury.

Tuesday: Tuesday is a Mars day, and just like the god of war, this is the time to tap into magick that calls for victory, strength, and courage, or if you are facing a challenge of any kind. This day of the week is for rebels and warriors. Keywords: Tuesday, Mars, strength/courage.

Wednesday: Wednesdays are wild and wacky days. They are for communication, change, cunning, and the arts. This is a Mercury day, and just like its patron god, this day is full of contradictions, change, good luck, and excitement. Keywords: Wednesday, Mercury, change/communication.

Thursday: Thursday is a Jupiter day. This is the day of the week for prosperity, abundance, and good health. Thursday is "Thor's day." This Norse god gave the day his name and many of his attributes, including strength and abundance. Keywords: Thursday, Jupiter, prosperity/health.

Friday: Friday belongs to Venus, both the planet and its namesake Roman goddess of love. This day is sacred to many other god/desses of love such as the Norse goddess who gave the day its name, Freya. This day of the week is for magickal topics such as love in all of its forms, birth, fertility, beauty, and romance. Keywords: Friday, Venus, love/romance.

Saturday: This day of the week got its name from the god of karma and time, Saturn. Traditionally Saturdays are great days for protection or banishing a negative situation, and they are generally a good time to clean up any magickal messes that you have been ignoring. Keywords: Saturday, Saturn, protection/banishing.

All-Purpose "Magick on the Fly" Charm Verse

Here is a "magick on the fly" charm verse that you can personalize for whatever your specific magickal need. In other words, you can turn this verse into an *all-purpose* spell.

Focus on whatever day of the week you happen to be in. Remember its qualities, focus on the keywords, and then be sure to know if the moon is waxing or waning. What do you need to increase or decrease? Consider your options, and choose your best magickal course of action. Now visualize what it is you are working toward, raise up your personal magickal energy/personal power, and send out a little energetic nudge into the universe. The repeat the following charm while you release that energy:

This type of magick is called "on the fly"
My instant spell will now soar to the sky.
This personal magickal energy I do now release
May my spell manifest correctly, with all possible speed!

Now take a moment and ground yourself. Draw a deep breath in through your nose and blow it slowly out through your mouth. Relax. Now go about your business, and enjoy the rest of your day.

Closing

The truth is we need to embrace the things we have in common as a community of magickal and metaphysical folks while at the same time respecting and enjoying the ideas, opinions, and qualities that make us different. When you look at a garden, you enjoy the overall scene; rarely do you focus only on one flowering plant. It is the mixture—the blending—of those colors, scents, heights, and textures. Diversity is what makes a garden enchanting, healing, nourishing, *and* beautiful. It even supports the natural health of the garden, as all the various plants work in harmony to repel harmful insects, draw pollinators, and replenish the soil. Diversity is complementary.

The same goes for our metaphysical and magickal community. When you approach differing opinions with an open mind, they aren't walls or roadblocks. They're opportunities to expand our horizons and see things we otherwise may have missed. Indeed, over the years we both have learned so much from other Witches and magick-minded folks. Exchanging ideas, trading stories, and sharing our personal experiences is the best way to grow, blossom, and thrive. This is true personally, but the same is true for our covens and spiritual circles, our greater spiritual community, and our planet. Let's just admit it, shall we? We need each other.

There are many magickal options and many paths to explore on your life's journey. You don't have to restrict yourself to one magickal style or path to learn something new. Look around *every Witch way*, be yourself, laugh, learn, and—most of all—follow your heart.

Blessed be,
Ellen and Tess

Ellen's Bibliography

Belanger, Michelle. *Ghost Hunter's Survival Guide.* Woodbury, MN: Llewellyn, 2009.

Cunningham, Scott. *Wicca in the Kitchen.* St. Paul, MN: Llewellyn, 2005.

Dugan, Ellen. *Book of Witchery.* Woodbury, MN: Llewellyn, 2009.

———. Cottage Witchery: Natural Magick for Hearth & Home. St. Paul, MN: Llewellyn, 2005.

———. *Garden Witchery.* St. Paul, MN: Llewellyn, 2003.

———. *How to Enchant a Man.* Woodbury, MN: Llewellyn, 2008.

———. *Natural Witchery.* Woodbury, MN: Llewellyn, 2007.

———. *Practical Prosperity Magick.* Woodbury, MN: Llewellyn, 2011.

———. *Practical Protection Magick.* Woodbury, MN: Llewellyn, 2014.

———. *Witches Tarot Companion.* Woodbury, MN: Llewellyn, 2012.

Moorey, Theresa. *Working with Psychic Protection.* New York: Sterling Publishing Company, 2007.

Whitehurst, Tess. *Magical Housekeeping.* Woodbury, MN: Llewellyn, 2010.

Tess's Bibliography

Campbell, Joseph. The Hero with a Thousand Faces (The Collected Works of Joseph Campbell). Novato, CA: New World Library, 2008.

Campbell, T. Colin and Thomas M. Campbell III. The China Study: The Most Comprehensive Study of Nutrition Ever Conducted and The Startling Implications for Diet, Weight Loss, and Long Term Health. Dallas: Benbella Books, 2005.

Collins, Terah Kathryn. The Western Guide to Feng Shui: Creating Balance, Harmony, and Prosperity in Your Environment. Carlsbad, CA: Hay House, 1996.

Devries, Mark, dir. *Speciesism: The Movie*. 2013. Film.

Eisenstien, Charles. Sacred Economics: Money, Gift, and Society in the Age of Transition. Berkeley, CA: Evolver Editions, 2011.

Fulkerson, Lee, dir. *Forks Over Knives*. Monica Beach Media, 2011. Film.

Illes, Judika. The Element Encyclopedia of Witchcraft: The Complete A-Z for the Entire Magical World. London: HarperElement, 2010.

Laszlo, Ervin. Science and the Akashic Field: An Integral Theory of Everything. Rochester, Vermont: Inner Traditions, 2004.

Linn, Denise. Soul Coaching: 28 Days to Discover Your Authentic Self. Carlsbad, CA: Hay House, 2003.

Martes, C. J. Akashic Field Affirmations: Heal the Past and Create Your Future. Lees Summit, MO: Martes Group, 2006.

Medici, Marina. *Good Magic.* New York: Fireside, 1989.

Melody. *Love Is in the Earth: A Kaleidoscope of Crystals.* Wheat Ridge, CO: Earth Love Publishing House, 1995.

Monson, Shaun, dir. *Earthlings: Make the Connection.* Nation Earth, 2005. Film.

Pollan, Michael. The Botany of Desire: A Plant's-Eye View of the World. New York: Random House, 2001.

Siefert, Jeremy, dir. *GMO OMG.* Compeller Pictures, 2013. Film.

Todeschi, Kevin J. *Edgar Cayce on the Akashic Records.* Virginia Beach: A.R.E. Press, 1998.

Virtue, Doreen. Healing with the Angels: How the Angels Can Assist You in Every Area of Your Life. Carlsbad, CA: Hay House, 1999.

Whitehurst, Tess. The Good Energy Book: Creating Harmony and Balance for Yourself and Your Home. Woodbury, MN: Llewellyn, 2012.

———. *Magical Clutter Clearing Boot Camp.* Los Angeles, CA: Tess Whitehurst, 2011.

———. Magical Housekeeping: Simple Charms and Practical Tips for Creating a Harmonious Home. Woodbury, MN: Llewellyn, 2010.

Made in the USA
San Bernardino, CA
09 March 2017